HEAVY TALES

AS LIVED BY JON ZAZULA

This book is dedicated to my children Danielle, Rikki and Blaire, who I thank for allowing me to live this dream in spite of it all. I thank you for your sacrifice. And to our dear parents Helen and Norman Zazula And Ramona and William Rutenberg who were taken from us too soon.

TABLE OF CONTENTS

INTRODUCTION

I'M NOT A SAINT AND I'm not a sinner. I'm just trying to get through each day just like you. I didn't ask for my life. It just happened. Very fortunate, I guess. At least I am sure it looked that way to most, but in truth no one knew the pain and depression that I was battling. Don't get me wrong, I'm a grateful man, but I am a textbook manic depressive and I've experienced many a manic wave where achievement and the spoils of success were my reality. I must say, however, those pits of depression were so dark and emotionally draining that at times it felt like hell on earth which plagued me on a more than wanted basis. Sometimes it became so deep there was no tunnel to get out from. Then like the sun shining through a rain cloud, all would be good again. Life would feel back to normal but not normal as you may imagine. Within the shortest amount of time to get grounded I got scooped up in a manic storm achieving, achieving, achieving as much as humanly possible.

I'm telling you this early on because everything you read in the pages that follow occurred during these massive mind-swings. I also have to tell you that if you don't believe in GOD you may find my mentioning His role in this story as a bit too much. Just know, I give GOD and my wife Marsha credit for every wonderful thing that has made this life so interesting. I feel like a pawn in his master game. Believe me, if you met me you would say, "Him? He did all of that?" You'd get what I'm saying right away. Don't be surprised when you read about all the mistakes and mishaps we had. In Baseball you're a star if you have a 350-batting average. I believe we had at least a 500 average with many grand slams.

Well, enjoy the book. I'm happy to share some of my long-kept tales with you. Thanks for letting me share my life. I hope it gives you the best accounting I can of the magical times in our Mega-Kingdom.

Jon Zazula-March 16th, 2019

CHAPTER 1

THE BEGINNING OF THE END

METALLICA'S *RIDE THE LIGHTNING* CAME out in July of 1984. When I had finally heard the finished product, I thought to myself, "They did it again those muthafuckas." It was amazing, simply amazing and I had no words for it. My wife Marsha and I had released their first album *Kill 'Em All* the previous July on our indie record label *Megaforce Records* but it seemed right to get a new one out so soon. It was proper to release their second offering within one year's time and let the fire blaze out of control. The entire sound had improved having producer Flemming Rasmussen on board which sonically elevated the album. The drums were bigger, the songs were tighter and the production went above and beyond expectations.

Within a short seven days of *Ride the Lightening's* release we had the Megaforce Records Artist Showcase concert in midtown Manhattan at the Roseland Ballroom which Marsha named *The Midsummer's Night Scream*. It was a diverse roster with Anthrax representing New York, Metallica representing the west coast and headliners Raven from New Castle, England, who at that time were riding high on the crest of the New Wave of British Heavy Metal (NWOBHM). Megaforce was holding the showcase because I had always been trying to prove a point as to how great these bands were, especially when there wasn't anyone in the industry who seemed to pay attention to me about this. The concert was going to change all of that. It was always our intention to have a tour centered around the release of an album and this was business as usual having released Metallica just a week earlier. It was turning into the biggest show Marsha and I had ever promoted and I believe there were over 3,000 tickets sold.

Everything was calculated back then, and it *had* to be in the pre-internet era. Promoting these kinds of heavy metal shows needed to be done on all the mediums we had available. There were no cellphones, no internet, no social media, no podcasts, nothing to promote on a wide scale approach like there is now. There was no heavy metal coverage or exposure in magazines, only glam and hair bands got that attention. The heavy metal community only had four college radio stations playing our music and two major stations, for a total of just six stations nationwide. These stations would only play our music from 12am-1am on Friday nights so it was extremely limiting to promote music or find new bands. There was nothing at that time similar to modern day promotion. We promoted this Megaforce showcase through radio advertisement, flyers and magazine ads. Marsha and I would go to bars and change all the flyers every two to three days and we would poster telephone polls as if we were running an election, with me running for my life. We did all of this to make sure people knew there was a concert coming up, so nobody could say they didn't know. Our main newspapers to advertise were *The Aquarian Weekly* in New Jersey and for Long Island and Queens we used *The Ear.* Marsha and I would start off with quarter-page ads and as the show came closer, would then take full-page ads, eventually moving onto centerfolds. We were always working hard on bringing people to the show. Honestly, sometimes it felt like the circus was coming to town with how much work we put in.

The night of the sold-out concert I stood outside and greeted almost every single person that walked through the door at the Roseland Ballroom; friends from Old Bridge, NJ, customers from our record store *Rock n Roll Heaven. Everyone* in the city was there that night and the line wrapped around for what seemed forever. Even Joey Ramone was in attendance. This was setting itself up to be a very special night and no one had even played yet.

Anthrax were the openers and they played a great set but it seemed there was some tension between them. There had always been tension among the band but it reached its boiling point by the end of their set, backstage. After an argument about tour jackets, their lead singer Neil quit right on the spot. We don't know what happened. He got pissed, walked away and no one from the band chased after him. Neil had always been an odd performer with a 50lb. metal mesh glove he wore that went from his hand to his elbow, fist-banging with it all night long. That alone was an amazing feat of endurance and it was quite a sight to behold.

Anthrax had just played their biggest hometown show to a sold out audience and their lead singer quit on the spot. Marsha and I ate our guts out that night. Even though Neil was a bit of an oddball, he had truly delivered on the first album vocally and we were knee deep in production of the band's next album. The greatest fear was to lose the momentum we had gained with the first album release and touring. We always believed everything was happening for a reason, hoping this situation was going to end up with a good outcome.

It wasn't going to be easy by any means, but we just believed in that divine intervention which always had us believing it would all somehow work out fine.

"GUESS WHO'S BACK IN TOWN TONIGHT!" screamed Metallica frontman James Hetfield as they took stage after Anthrax. James had his Flying V guitar strapped on and the place erupted. You knew from the audience it was something special. For me, it was like seeing the Grateful Dead live for the first time. I had tears running down my face. I couldn't hide it as the band's intro music began to play. As the intro continued, which I had given to the band to use from my love of Ennio Morricone's soundtracks, I felt such an overwhelming amount of pride for my boys. Seeing all the bands on stage made me feel like a father watching his children graduate Summa Cum Laude. I was so fucking proud of what I was seeing and the crowd loved it. It was a sight to behold!

During the Metallica set I had noticed some people hanging around the audience. *Q-Prime Artist Management* co-founder Cliff Burnstein, *Elektra Records* CEO Bob Krasnow and his young *A&R* man Michael Alago were all there at this concert. I had met Michael a few times already and I was always in talks with having an Elektra/Megaforce deal but no one was ever interested at the time. Now they were there for Metallica and I had a feeling they wanted me out of the way; Out of the way with the band, out of the way with my label, and out of the way with my management. I wanted to stick my head in the sand. I got the vibe it was a very unwelcomed world I was in. Internally I wished them the best, but when we approached each other in the hall I turned around and walked away. The very next morning Metallica met with Bob Krasnow, brought to him by Michael Alago and soon signed a record deal. They switched management to Q-Prime, who managed several big name acts at the time one of which was Def Leppard. This all happened without my knowledge.

It hurt me when I got the news because I was destined, in my mind, for bigger things than where we currently were with Metallica. I was going to ride with them until the end of time. I never saw an end to this trip. Marsha and I felt we had made a family. I felt stupid for feeling like this. Looking back, I feel like I should've held on to the band, that I should've fought harder to keep the partnership alive. But I knew that you can't keep a band who doesn't want you, so we made our agreements and went our separate ways. At the time I felt majorly betrayed. The strength of a major label would have propelled all of us. We would have grown together, but when Metallica left the management company it was the end of that dream. We always wanted them to be on a major label, We wanted all our bands to, but hoped they would stay with us for management and direction.

But it was too late. Who do you go to when there's no money or when you have a problem? You go to the label or you go to your manager to speak to the label on your behalf. Since we were operating as both, we had to take all the hits, all the frustration and all the expenses so we felt if we had a major label attached it would only help get the band bigger. The touring, promotion, advertisements, record distribution, and getting the bands on the radio, it would just elevate the bands and skyrocket them to success. As it turns out, Elektra were already talking to them prior to the show. The seeds were already being planted for this underneath our noses without any knowledge of it. When Metallica left us we were broken hearted but that's the way this business works. It's anguish after anguish. We could have been much more brutal to each other during our separation but the respect we had thankfully didn't allow for it to reach that level. The settlement I was

11

given by the band was something I couldn't turn down and was much needed to help Megaforce grow its other acts. Plus, we agreed on having the Megaforce Records logo on the next two releases which was a good move for us. I'll stand firmly and say I don't believe their career would've been any different had we stayed on managing them. They still would've become the biggest band in the world, but I do admit their new management did a more than remarkable job over the years and I highly respect their fine work. It surpassed even my wildest imagination.

Metallica's drummer Lars Ulrich always had a goal for his band. He wanted to be like Def Leppard or AC/DC. Superstars. From the second you met Lars he already had bigger dreams and aspirations for the band. He had a certain drive even at 20 years old that set him aside from other people in the scene. He not only wanted to be like the superstars he loved like in Deep Purple, he wanted to *be them*. Growing up in the spotlight, as his father was a professional tennis player, he was destined for greatness. The stars and the sun shine on Lars at all times. He has a natural sense of leadership and intuition far beyond his years and it was evident from the very moment you spoke with him. He has a brilliant mind for business and this was just another business decision made on their part.

The show was a big turnaround for all these bands, not just Metallica. Sometime after Neil left Anthrax, we made a deal with Island Records where we were kept on as their managers. Raven made a deal with Atlantic the same year as well and we also got to remain their managers. We had a partner post-Metallica at *Crazed Management* named Tony Incigeri, one of my favorite people ever on earth. Unfortunately, our vision for Raven was quite different and we couldn't agree on a direction for the band. Subsequently, he didn't understand what

I saw in Anthrax nor understood why I was investing so much time with them. It was breaking my heart and I couldn't look at what was happening to Raven once they signed to Atlantic Records. What we decided to do, Tony Incigeri and I, was he took Raven and I took Anthrax and we parted ways right before we finished the second Anthrax album in 1985. I went through hell during this time period because for me, Raven were one of my favorite bands of all time and this would be a permanent departure.

Thankfully Anthrax guitarist Scott Ian and I became extremely close during that sad time. All our ideas bounced off each other. It's something special I've always had with him. Although Neil had left the band, Scott and I continued our quest for his replacement. I was already used to this and thankful we were going through it together figuring out the next move. As we continued on with Anthrax, we had renewed excitement with the signing by Chris Blackwell to Island Records. Brainstorming after Neil left the band and reorganizing would not be too difficult.

The Showcase at Roseland changed everything overnight for all of us. All the bands on the bill got a major label record deal soon after the show. Metallica going off to sign with Elektra, Raven with Atlantic and Anthrax through a joint venture we signed with Island Records. Marsha and I had started this whole thing out of a flea market in New Jersey no more than two and a half years before and now things had changed. Our heads were spinning. Throughout the years to follow we would face even greater challenges filled with success, sadness and even death. Together Marsha and I would build a dynasty out of a little flea market, experiencing both the agony and ecstasy of it all.

CHAPTER 2

DREAMS OF DALI

I ALWAYS HAD DREAMS OF A Salvador Dali-like figure when I was little. My dreams had me on a gondola-like boat filled with gems, going up an elevator made of glass and gold. I'd be rising from the ocean up a cliff going to his house on the edge of the sea and meeting him there. These dreams would go on until I was at least 19 years old. I always remembered that boat and elevator ride in those elaborate dreams in my youth.

I grew up in a house of fear. The anxiety level was always at 10 and there was no place to hide. I remember once trying to hide under the bed one day and my father couldn't reach me with his hands so he went and got a broom and started harpooning me with it while I was trying to avoid getting seriously pulverized. When I jumped out from hiding, he slammed me with the metal broom so hard that it bent in half. This was an example of everyday life at 1236 Burke Ave. in the Bronx. My mother, a wonderful, brilliant woman, would never get in the middle when Dad raged on, causing me to disrespect her for staying married to him. She was a social worker who worked as an Administrator at a nursing home and died a terrible death at a young age from diabetes.

The insanity in my house was at epic proportions yet there was always music playing in the air. From my folks I developed a solid understanding of music. I was taught at a young age what sounds were made by what instruments and how these instruments would blend and work together to form a body of music. As crazy as my father was, he would, as much as he could, take me to see the NY Philharmonic and operas at the old Metropolitan Opera House. This was never enough for me and it started my journey of loving music at quite a young age. I dreamt of escaping the madhouse and then the day came.

In an attempt to protect myself during one incident I pulled a butcher knife from the kitchen drawer and held it to my father's neck until his rage simmered down. This act was considered unforgivable, so sadly at the age of 16 I left my brothers Evan, who was 12, and Robert, who was 10 years old, behind to fend for themselves, something I felt I had to do. Now please understand this was the 60's. It was an easy time to be a hippie and take a train down to the East Village in New York City where I could blend in with my other brothers and sisters of love and find places to crash out for the night. It was the time of the Vietnam War back in 67-69. Everything was "helter skelter" in downtown NYC and I fit right in.

Due to my leaving home, I lived on and off the streets in those days. No one knew what I was doing because I went to school daily and then ventured off to the Village in Manhattan or the "Wall" on Pelham Pkwy and White Plains Rd in the Bronx where there were nights I had to sleep on a park bench because there was no other choice. There was even a 24-hour restaurant in the East Village I would visit that had a friendly bathroom to use. I remember holding it in with all my might until I got to Hodi's on the corner of St. Mark's Place many times. That place was always there for me.

One of my greatest life changing experiences came from a night I was sleeping on a park bench in a playground that I think was called Tompkin's Square Park off Avenue A in the East Village. A man 20 years my senior sat next to me. He was homeless but unusually well dressed. It was 3am and I was very stoned but had no fear of this stranger who happened to pick my bench to sit on. I had no fear because I had nothing to give this man. I honestly believed that if he were a thief he wouldn't even bother to put me on his radar. I was broke and it showed. It wouldn't even be worth the time or effort to rob me.

We started talking to each other and I remember he looked like Jimi Hendrix and in our conversation he introduced himself to me by giving me his business card where on one side it said "Rev." and the other side had these words boldly printed on it: "NOTHING TO IT BUT TO DO IT." For some crazy reason I walked around with that card for years. It became my mantra. I still utter the words today. I never officially returned home and before I was 18 I had my own apartment on Villa Ave in the Bronx off the Grand Concourse.

Now here's the sugar coated version:

I had an average size family growing up in the Bronx, just my two younger brothers, Evan and Robert, my parents and my grandmother living all together in the same apartment in the Eastchester Housing projects on Burke Ave. My parents never put anything on me to have a lot of responsibility helping raise my younger brothers. I never spent much time with them anyway. I was always on my own, hanging with my friends from school or locked up by myself in my room listening to music.

I had a very stern but loving relationship with my father but he was a man who was afraid of responsibility and growth. He was afraid of ever taking a challenge. I always fought with him as a youth to buy a house instead of living in an apartment, even though he had the money. But my words were in vain. In truth, I actually hated him and used him as the picture of the man I never wanted to grow up to be. My mother, on the other hand, was a strong, brilliant woman. But unfortunately her health and sight suffered from debilitating diabetes, holding her back and taking her life too soon.

My mother's sisters, Aunt Faye and Aunt Bobbi, knew my love and passion for baseball cards but they wanted to see me explore my interest in music so they decided to buy me some records thinking this could be a start to another collection. They bought me six records but none of them were the ones I asked for. I was disappointed because I wanted the new single by Bobby Rydell, "Volare" and I got another single by him, "Butterfly Baby" instead. As time passed, I listened to all six of those records over and over again and they entertained me for a while.

When I was six years old I went to buy my first album with Chubby Checker's "The Twist" on it but it was sold out so I bought his other album, "For Twisters Only". Once I got home I found out the "Twist" wasn't on the album, which taught me the invaluable lesson that you had to actually read the back cover because you might not get the song you wanted. But I twisted away to that album anyway. Music at that time was special for me. I dug the hell out of it. My mother had an amazing voice and would walk around singing her brains out. She was always singing whether it was in the middle of the street or the supermarket and oh GOD, she would embarrass me constantly. Her professional claim to fame was when she recorded a demo of "Little White Lies" but her version never made it anywhere.

I bought my first drum set when I was 13 years old with money I earned from waxing cars and delivering newspapers with a shopping cart because I didn't even own a bicycle. The main music I would first play on the drums was a lot of British Invasion stuff like the Beatles, The Dave Clark 5 and Trini Lopez from the states. I wore the grooves out of that Trini Lopez "Live at PJ's" album. When I wasn't playing music I was listening to it. All I would do was hang out with kids from school who were also into music. We would listen to records at each other's houses. In the mid 60's, when I was fourteen, my friends and I would cut school and go downtown to watch live bands as much as we could. Our favorites at the time were the Murray the K shows where we saw acts such as an upcoming artist named Stevie Wonder. We saw The Young Rascals do all their early stuff, Mitch Ryder and the Detroit Wheels, the McCoys performing "Hang on Sloopy," and countless others. I even got to see Cream's first US concert at the Murray the K show down at the RKO on 58th street in Manhattan.

By the time I was fifteen my interests changed and it was The Grateful Dead, Jefferson Airplane and LSD that became my biggest influences. Jerry Garcia from the Grateful Dead, to me, was the ultimate guitar player and watching the band live was like going to a bible meeting. At the time they would perform music that created a psychokinetic energy which would take you on a journey ... and I loved going on that journey with them. For me the Dead died when Jerry passed away. It'll never be the same.

The summer I graduated high school I had seen Cream at the Village Theater on 2nd Ave. in New York City, prior to it becoming the Fillmore East. I was so impressed at the power and heaviness of this three-man group that they, too, became a great musical influence in my life. Although it wasn't called "Heavy Metal," it sure was heavy. The thing I remember about that show was my balls vibrated from Jack Bruce's bass and going deaf for three whole days before I could hear again. My interest in heavier music continued with seeing Led Zeppelin and Jeff Beck Group live at the Fillmore. It was the sound of the Marshall amps that really ripped my head off. The sound was amazing and revolutionary at the time.

During college I met someone who was working for Columbia Records Club and she would give me some extra records for free every once in a while, just great things that were returned from other customers. These reject records included Deep Purple, Ted Nugent and UFO, which I loved, but all the while I still remained a loyal Dead fan.

I got married after college and had my first child Danielle four years later. At the time I was selling life insurance to support my family and lived a very generic life in Yonkers, New York in Westchester County. In the '70s I would visit my friend at his house. He was dating a girl named Marsha. She was the sweetest thing, but on our first meeting she gave me a rough time and hated me because of my arrogance and ego. Sometime later we realized we were both jazz freaks and she knew her music very well, so we bonded. Marsha loved Gato Barbieri and Wayne Shorter and I was head over heels in love with Roland Kirk, so through this a friendship developed and it became evident we had a special connection. We became friends fairly quickly and began going to shows with our significant others. After a few years my first marriage ended in divorce. I thought of Marsha a lot but I didn't know how to reach her because our lives had taken us in different directions and to my knowledge she had already moved on to a whole new planet.

One day my friend Ruthie said to me, "You know, Jon, I ran into Marsha the other day and she's recently single. She gave me her number. I told her I'd give it to you but you don't have to call." I rushed to the phone and called right away, making a date with Marsha right there.

Our first date was on a Friday night at a place called The Rocker Room, a seafood restaurant by day and a rock club by night. It was a very cool scene in New York at the time. They had Elvis Costello, Blondie, The Ramones and The Cars playing through the restaurant speakers. I didn't consider that music punk. I didn't consider the Clash punk either. It was pop music to me. After the date we went back to my apartment. We didn't do anything but hang out and listen to music. When Saturday came and she needed to go home I talked her out of leaving and she stayed an additional night. Sunday night it rained so bad the highways started flooding, so I couldn't take Marsha home for safety reasons. She ended up staying with me after the first date Friday, Saturday and now Sunday without any escape in sight. Then on Monday she made it to work. That night I had to go pick up my brother at the airport. After I picked him up we drove over to her house in Queens at 7pm and I started packing up her things as I talked her into moving in with me. She was having this conversation with me as her clothes were going through the door. We've never been apart since. I was instantly in love, head over heels with her the second we reunited.

Three months later Marsha's cousin was getting married in Dallas and I finagled an invitation to the wedding. The truth is the thought of Marsha being away for two to three days was unbearable. While at the airport in Dallas on the escalator, I asked Marsha if she would like to go to this wedding as an engaged person since we'd be with her whole family. "Yeah okay, that sounds cool, why not?" Marsha replied to me. It still makes me laugh how easy everything happened. It didn't startle her how quickly I proposed. Being friends for such a long time and sharing so much mutual respect for each other, our first date was a culmination of those feelings that had been felt but never acted on. Marsha wanted to be with someone who cared and respected her and my actions only spoke in that manner. We were both 28, living on our own, self-supported, and working full time. I had already been married and had my daughter Danielle. I felt it was an appropriate time to ask her. Marsha saw what a devoted husband I was in my first marriage and what a good father I was, so that spoke to my character.

On arrival, Marsha's family made it official and we announced our engagement.

We got married on August 5th, 1979 at the 5th Ave. Hotel in New York City. Marsha's mother passed away at a very young age from cancer before we had reconnected, and her father was deeply devastated. He didn't know how to make a wedding for Marsha that would make her mother proud, even though she wouldn't be there, so we got married at the same place Marsha's sister had gotten married four years earlier. Her father went to the banquet manager to take out the files and photos from the previous wedding and to repeat the performance, only the color scheme would be yellow instead of blue this time.

I was losing interest in selling life insurance and my salary was on a fast decline as well. It was time for a career change, and in the job interviews I had taken, Wall Street kept coming up. So off to Wall Street I went.

CHAPTER 3

FROM HELL TO ROCK N ROLL HEAVEN

I HAD GRADUATED SCHOOL FOR MY National Association of Securities Dealers license and was hired at an investment banking firm on Wall Street in July of 1980. Marsha got pregnant so we moved to Old Bridge, NJ and bought our first home and on March of the following year we had our daughter Rikki. While working on Wall Street I was trading stocks and building portfolios for investors. I was there a year and took an interest in commodity trading because we had a trading room next door where everyone was getting rich in the gold rush. That's the time when everyone was going wild over gold and I saw kids that never even went to college making $17k a week, *every single week*. It was driving me crazy. I felt that I needed to be a part of that money making so I became friends with those guys and eventually was asked to join them.

After gold had its run, those guys asked me to come with them to work in a regular commodity house to trade items such as Pork Belly's and sugar. I took a job there to learn the business and was successful in sales because of my hunch. When Fidel Castro tried to open relationships with the U.S., I felt something was suspicious without any statistical clue. I believed he was having economic problems in his country. I then heard there may be a problem with Cuba's sugar production. Sugar at that time was about 2 cents a pound. Sugar contracts were extremely inexpensive and gave you much leverage if the price would fluctuate. I had predicted the price would go up soon. My hunch was unfounded, but as soon as I mentioned this, the price magically rose one penny. This was followed by sugar again going up an additional two cents, which already meant the price had doubled and I believed it had the potential of going 33 cents or more. Every time sugar moved 1 cent, your contract was worth $1,100 more. Of course I had no charts or anything to back up these claims, as it was just a gut feeling. I don't remember where sugar wound up but it may have been 44 cents a pound and a lot of people made a whole lot of money, but not my clients. Somehow, they broke even at best, which caused much disdain between my clients and the people who traded for us. It was definitely time to move on again.

It was decided I would continue in commodities but after seeing the madness of trading in that market and the risks involved, it was time to find something more conservative so off I went again. This time my attention was focused on what was to be called "strategic minerals" and the mineral chosen to invest in was Tantalum. We would get investors of the company to stockpile the rare metal tantalum that is used for submarines and weapons manufacturing. With the Cold War happening and the U.S involved in the arms race at the time, I believed trading these metals would be a great alternative in investment. I was leery about this at first but it sounded logical and an ingenious way to invest some money. The company grew over a period of four and a half months and was quite successful. There was only one problem.

On Monday, July 13th, 1981, after returning to work from a wonderful weekend trip with Marsha and some of my friends in Montauk, NY, I was arrested by the Attorney General Robert Abrams of the state of New York. The police had ripped out all the phones from the wall and all 32 of us were under arrest for wire fraud. It turned out all the metal we were purchasing was under 99% pure and apparently had little value unless it had been over 99%. Even though the company purchased tantalum that was 98%-99% pure it was not the investment grade as we had promised. The sales force had been told by the company owners that the tantalum was being stored in insured government warehouses confirming it was indeed investment grade but that meant nothing. I'd like to say I didn't know about it, but the person who I am today admits I must've turned a blind eye.

It was 98 degrees that day in the paddy wagon with no air conditioning which made for a miserable trip to the police station. I remember using the roll of toilet paper on my bench as a pillow so I could sleep that night in my cell. Marsha was home with our daughter and tried calling me at the office earlier in the day without being able to check in on me. After I didn't come home at my normal time she figured I went out with the guys from the office. She wasn't too concerned about it until she was watching Fox news at 6 o'clock, which was a broadcast she normally didn't watch. They had a flash across the screen about a commodities firm that'd been closed down due to fraudulent trading and her ears perked up. On the screen she saw the 32 men being marched by the police out of the offices in handcuffs with books and newspapers covering our faces. She remembered what I was wearing to work that day and recognized me in my beige pants and burgundy shirt and flipped out. It wasn't until much later that evening, at, when she finally heard from me and I told her about the arrest. There was no posting bond and I was told jury selection would take six months which meant everybody had to show up every single day sitting in a courtroom plus another year of trial on top of that. My lawyer came up to me and confirmed I would not be able to afford this. Since we owned a home I couldn't qualify for a public defender, so I gave up my stamp collection and everything I owned to my lawyer to put towards our ever-increasing bill. He told me, "Jon, no one's ever going to believe you didn't know. You're never going to win this trial. You are too intelligent. People just aren't going to believe that you were so stupid." So, I took responsibility for my actions and pleaded guilty, ending up serving time at the mercy of the court for six months at a halfway house in Newark, NJ.

They took my license so I couldn't drive and I was only allowed to work if someone could get me there. The halfway house is where ex-inmates go to make the transition between prison and the real world. There was only one payphone there for the 48 people who just got out of prison waiting to do their halfway time which could've been half a year or more. When everybody came out of prison and into the halfway house they all ran to that payphone to call their sweethearts to tell them they were coming home soon. Imagine a line of 12 heavy duty ex-criminals trying to patiently wait for the phone and for permanent sunshine outside. I was the only guy not fresh from prison on the entire line, and the other guys in the facility weren't very friendly. Word of advice; don't share rooms in halfway houses with people who don't like snorers. I'm a snorer and a big person. I ended up tossed upside down in my mattress a few times by the other men I shared living quarters with. Luckily no one put a pillow over my head and ended me. One night while sleeping I was listening to "The Birthday Eve" by Loudness (from Japan) on my Walkman and I woke up without it. From that point I brought nothing of any value into that house. Marsha would have to come pick me up in Newark all the way from Old Bridge which was 30 miles south. There were guidelines to being able to leave the halfway house, such as having a job, so I found a job selling paper for a computer supply corporation paying me $250 a week. My cousin Harold helped me get the job and if it wasn't for him I probably wouldn't have been able to get one because of my criminal record.

Marsha would drive to the halfway house every morning to pick me up, drop me off at work, go back home and take care of the baby, then go pick me up from work, drop me off in Newark and go back home for the night in Old Bridge. This went on every day starting at six in the morning for Marsha and Rikki. We were fortunate because after a month they let me have my driving rights back. At first it was no weekends at home, then a few weekends, and then I was only allowed to go home on the weekends if I worked, which meant I had to find a way to work on the weekends. Financially, not being able to work hurt us badly. We had to sell one of our two cars and budget ourselves much tighter. I had a house and a brand new baby and basically Marsha's father would help us weekly on groceries. It would eat at my groin that this was going on but what could I do? Let my family starve? I didn't make enough money to make ends meet or pay my mortgage, it was horrible.

One weekend when I had a Saturday off, we went to an indoor flea market in East Brunswick, NJ off of Route 18 and saw a little music stand that sold cassettes, 8-tracks and records. They had this little space in the corner. It was nothing but it had a constant flow of people walking past it who always bought records. Marsha and I had always collected records and owned some great rarities, so I went to him and asked if he would ever consider buying records from us. They told me they weren't interested but suggested someone else who might be. So, I went to another guy at the market and told him I had $150 worth of King Biscuit "Flower Hour" albums that I had gotten from my Columbia Records friend in college and a Styx collection for sale which he ended up buying. Marsha lent me $30 because I had a plan in my mind that I could turn the $180 into a profit by buying collectible records to sell. We went back to the first guy and asked if we could rent out the little extra space he had, telling him we would just focus on collectibles, imports, picture discs and rarities. He charged us $10 for Fridays, $10 Saturdays and $5 for Sundays since they closed early for a total of $25 for the three days the flea market was open. It was no space at all but the little corner was all we needed. It was my ultimate dream to be able to pay for my own family's groceries. All I had to do was clear $70 each weekend. Remember we started with just $180.00 in inventory. On December 7th, 1981, Pearl Harbor Day, Marsha and I went to buy our records and get ready for the long weekend. I decided to call our store *Rock n Roll Heaven* because the concept I had was to solely specialize in music by dead people. John Lennon, Jim Morrison and Jimi Hendrix. We'd pay homage in some way to artists that were dead or gone.

We were placing picture discs upon the back of empty boxes as our display and were constantly talking to people at the market about what we were selling. We managed to get very rare picture discs for about $20 and we sold them for $50 based on prices we saw elsewhere at over $100 for the same item. To make $30 on a piece is a big deal, it's a cause for celebration, but

27

it wasn't happening that night. We sat there all night but no one was interested. Customers would talk to us about Pat Benatar, The Kinks' "Father Christmas" and other things we had, but no one was buying a single thing. We sat there looking at the money we spent without a single sale and thought to ourselves, "What the hell did we just do?" There used to be a television show, "I married Joan," with Joan getting in so much trouble and it was all about her husband dealing with her insane actions. Marsha would sing to me the theme song, "I married Jon, what a joy, what a boy, what a life!" to sort of just playfully poke fun at me. As the end of the day came closer I felt like my head was going to explode. I backed up against the post of the stand next to ours, LK Babyland, and held onto their curtains as I pounded my head. As I was feeling all the pressure I thought to myself, "Lord, what am I going to do now? I'm out $180, how am I going to feed my family? What the hell am I doing? Did I do one thing right in my life?" I felt a powerful higher force shove me against the chest, almost making me trip backwards. I felt like I was falling back through the wall as I let out a loud, "FUCK!" and all of a sudden I felt really good. I felt very nervous, very emotional and sat down all confused. Marsha saw me light up and she was happy seeing me happy. We have parallel circuits; we function on the same electrical current. Just like Christmas tree lights, when one bulb is out all the lights go out. It was an hour before closing and someone bought a 12" "Sad Wings of Destiny" Judas Priest picture disc record for $50, which was a very rare piece. This was followed by several other sales and we ended up making a few dollars that weekend.

After that encounter, with what I believed was Divine Intervention, things seemed to pick up. At that time, I was at the bottom of the barrel, couldn't feed my family, doing time, wasn't granted weekends at home yet from the halfway house and was barely seeing my kids. I remember the pain in my head leaning against the pole when I was shoved and fell down. From then on I felt very fortunate with the decisions I would make. I was a person that had drive. I used to joke around and think I was Noah, when he's told to build the ark. I felt like GOD said, "Go, you're on the right track, hang in there and what you sow you will reap." I didn't get it in words, I just got it with a big blast. It wasn't a big thing with *Gone with the Wind* music, just a tap on the shoulder. GOD came to me when I was as down as a man could be. I was having a nervous twitch due to the stress I had in my head. I was a mess, but things felt differently now.

That next Monday we had to order the same picture discs from where we got them to set up for the upcoming Friday and do it all over again. We weren't really completing the dream of feeding the family yet but we could see it in our sight. What ended up being our biggest break was during the holiday season when people were looking for different things to buy their parents and partners. People started stopping by to look at the picture discs as they were eye-catching gifts. Jim Kozlowski from Important Records made us aware of all the important vinyl our customers may be interested in the following week. He recommended Genesis, "Selling England by the Pound," Public Image boxset, just great stuff like Thin Lizzy, Gary Moore, things that were unknown to us. He eventually became our contact for heavy metal with imports coming in every week.

Marsha would go with whatever money she had in her pocket, plus gas and tolls for her car with the baby in tow making the drive to buy the imports from Old Bridge, NJ to Kennedy Airport two hours away and back again. She would make this trip every single Thursday to get ready for the three-day weekend of work. During work on Fridays I would see her coming in with a baby in one hand and a shopping cart wagon full of record boxes in the other. GOD knows how much they weighed. She would go into that Important Distribution warehouse, inspect the records, make sure they were the right ones and then buy them. Sometimes records would show up that weren't on our original list and Marsha would be smart enough to snag them for customers. Those included Motorhead's "Beer Drinkers EP," their gold vinyl release of "No Sleep 'Till Hammersmith," and Angel Witch. She was a very good buyer. Eventually she picked up a magazine called *Kerrang!* and we brought that to the store. Initially no one cared or knew what it was, but soon everybody bought them all up. We would get issues for $2 each and sell them for $3 and the demand for them became huge. Soon everyone from the store would read the magazines and ask us to bring this record from England, or that record from Germany or Japan so we would go to Important and they would buy it for us. We also bought great American bands too, locals like The Rods or Y&T from California, and NY's Twisted Sister. The whole thing exploded though with the New Wave of British Heavy Metal. Bands like Iron Maiden, Raven, Venom and Girlschool were heavily demanded by our clients. We were getting turned on to great bands by these kids so we learned a lot from them as well. First of all, you couldn't tell the customers about the music unless you knew what you were talking about. In fact, some of the stuff we wanted to bring in the store, even Important Records wasn't aware of. We were assisting the company to expand the type of heavy metal they were importing. At first we started with small orders, but soon we were buying records like a chain store such as Sam Goodie and The Wiz, loads and loads of records. Instead of just buying two records of a band, we knew our clients would want more so we bought a massive amount of Accept or Michael Schenker, for example. Sometimes we'd buy as many as 200 albums a piece when there was a new release.

Rock n Roll Heaven would send out letters to all our customers thanking them for their support and reporting what albums were coming soon. We would put these out every month with the addresses the customers would leave in the store, paying for the postage which we really couldn't afford to do. Our friends Gabriele, Brian and Maria would help us get these letters to the customers. Thanks for stuffing and stamping envelopes on our living room floor. At one point we made a shirt of all the people who died and went to "Rock n Roll Heaven" and if you wore the shirt into the store you would get 10% off. You would see the flea market loaded with people wearing our shirts which had other shoppers thinking, "What the hell is *Rock n Roll Heaven?*" There was a following of *Rock n Roll Heaven* fans in Old Bridge, NJ which solidified and legitimized our store.

In a short time we were even asked by our customers to bring over this band Anvil from Canada, to perform a local show since their new album "Metal on Metal" was sort of groundbreaking for the scene. I don't remember if I just reached out to their lead singer, "Lips," or to their manager or Attic Records which was their record company about bringing them over into America. We had the concert at the back of the flea market in an empty auditorium with no seats, just an empty floor with a small low stage in August on Friday the 13th, 1982. That was it, nothing else. We went to the owners of the flea market and asked if they could rent us this space for the show we wanted to do. They weren't interested so we pestered them until they finally gave in. The market's management gave us a whole list of things we couldn't do, a strict time schedule, incorporating the flea market with our advertisement for the show to promote them. The rules included no alcohol at all, no smoking cigarettes or pretty much anything, and we had an 11pm curfew. We had to bring extra power for the electricity because their power wasn't strong enough for the bands' equipment. Since there were no seats Marsha went to a church and rented out their chairs, creating a schematic to label and number every seat with stickers. The day of the show the band gets there with their gear and they go to plug in and we find out the auditorium doesn't have enough power. We blew out the power in the whole flea market and they were not too thrilled about it. Someone we knew had a friend who had a generator truck. The company was called *Paul Sound* and they came in with a power generator and plugged us in so we could have sound and power, costing us $600. We never anticipated that cost in the show's budget. By the way nobody sat down the entire night, the chairs got pushed back and broken while the kids were all upfront pounding on the stage. We didn't even have a barricade to separate the band and the audience. The metal kids from Old Bridge wanted to make the band feel respected so they brought couches, chairs, lamps and tables to create a backstage area for the band to lounge in. We gave the guy who sold hot dogs at the flea market the food concession to be able to sell food and cold drinks at the venue. In return he had to feed the bands since we wanted them all to be fed. A local band, Prey, opened up that night for Anvil. They were a cross between a cover band and an original band that really represented the night well. The kids went berserk with the bands. We told the Old Bridge crowd that if they wanted front row seats they had to each sell 20 tickets. All these kids went out with their 20 tickets and started selling them, coming back for another 20. With the money we got from selling tickets we were able to pay for an immigration lawyer to bring Anvil across the border. There wasn't any real security at the show but the kids knew that if they ever wanted to see a live show in their backyard again they had to live by the rules. The crowd from Old Bridge sort of ruled everybody, keeping them calm and cool. After the show I don't know if we felt an instant urge to want to do another show but if we did it would be for these great metal fans. I want it to be known that while I was promoting and booking this shows, I still lived in that halfway house. In order to make phone calls I would lie and tell the inmates I was booking Kool and the Gang concerts when it was actually Anvil and preparing for future shows, like Venom and Raven. On that payphone all the shows were planned, put together and executed and I got away with it. Attending those shows was tricky because I was supposed to be back at the halfway house by 9pm and sometimes 6:30pm for the curfews. So the Federal Marshall who was in charge of the place escorted me to the shows personally and I was a real pain in his ass. Once we were short on production staff and the Federal Marshall had to help out with lights when the light man never showed up for the gig. I had to demonstrate that I wasn't doing any illegal activities outside of the place so he had to come along for the ride. He came to the shows and saw that I was involved in something positive, which was great for me because him being there and getting to know me got me released about 2 months early from the halfway house. He felt I was a righteous man.

At that point we were very close to Raven and their record company Neat Records who were very interested in having them play their first American gig. We set up a Halloween show in 1982 dubbed "The Halloween

Headbanger's Ball" way before that show even aired on MTV. The fans asked for us to bring Anvil back so we added them to the bill. We wanted The Rods to headline but they wanted a lot of money so we went and asked Riot from New York if they wanted to play since they were local favorites with their new album "Restless Breed." That's how we met Jeff Rowland since he was representing Riot back then. This time around we held the concert at the St. George Theater by the Staten Island Ferry. We met a young man by the name of Dean Holterman whose parents ran Holterman's Bakery, which was huge in Staten Island. He wanted to be involved in promoting in a very big way and it was his friends at the St. George Theater who gave us a great deal. It was through that deal we connected and started working together. So Dean and the Zazulas teamed up with Marsha's sister and brother-in-law and we promoted the first annual Halloween Headbanger's Ball. That was the worst and most stressful night of my life. It was an old theater with leaks, the place was probably condemned, the event was approved just one day before our show. Once again we had no security for the now 1,100 people that showed up. We had motorcycle people there because we were going to drive a headless biker across the stage on a Harley. There was a fire breathing dragon built for the front lobby that blew grey and green smoke. With no ladder we had no way of rigging the lights and there was nothing in the theater. Somebody went down to the basement where there was this big hole in the floor and found a 50 ft. ladder. I had to pay someone money I didn't have to get on that ladder and rig and hang lights so I could have a show. I didn't know you had to hire an electrician to be there to turn on the power since there was no power. I had no limits for backstage guests: we catered for 50 and over 200 girls ended up backstage.

There were more girls there for Riot than I had ever seen in my life. We created special event t-shirts which we wanted printed orange on black shirts but it turned out to be black on an orange shirt, how gross. So we told the crowd that if they bought that event shirt and wore it to the store they would get 10% off merchandise because we had to raise the price of the shirt to match the Riot t-shirt price according to their contract.

There were three fights I broke up at the show, screaming at them to pounce on me instead of bashing each other. It was a really wild night. There was a drunk fellow who climbed up on the PA and started shaking it, almost making it fall down, which could've really hurt some people. I didn't know what to do since I didn't have any security so I went towards him and grabbed him by the seams of his pants. I lifted him up and took him off the PA. Then the drunk guy turned around in a fighting stance ready to nail me and kick my ass. Out of the crowd flying from midair came my friend from Old Bridge, Ray Dill, to save my ass. Ray's not the tallest guy, but had a strong rugged build and can more than handle himself in any ugly situation. He gave him a bear hug around the chest and pulled him in, turning the guy purple in a second. Anvil's drummer Robb Reiner was playing a drum solo during this whole thing and the guy was trying to get out of the bear hug. I felt safe where I was now, thank GOD for Ray Dill. During the incident the drums start going, "boomboom-boomboom-boomboomboomboom-Let's go!" and the guy miraculously starts getting into the drum solo and lost focus on what he was doing. Ray let him go and gave me a high-five as he vanished into the audience.

A young Scott Ian and Danny Lilker, of Anthrax, were at that show, always hanging out in every corner, sneaking in backstage, I don't know how they got there all the time. It was an undeniably insane show from start to finish which drove me nuts by how quick we had moved from a flea market show to a theater concert in just two months.

One day at the store an older regular came in who had just came back from California. He was into race cars and while attending an event in San Francisco he decided to check out a local heavy metal show. At the show he bought a demo and a live cassette and brought them over to the store for me to listen to. He told me I would love them. "Jonnnny you gotta hear this!" he said to me at the store, but the thing is I had never played demos at the store without listening to them first. I would take demo tapes and cassettes home and if they had a certain quality I would then play them at the store. I would screen bands for my customers, but he insisted, so we put it on the little broken speakers we had at the store and within the first song I instantly thought to myself, "what the fuck?? This is fucking amazing."

I looked at the demo tape and its name written in all black: *MetallicA*- "No Life 'Til Leather".

CHAPTER 4

THE YOUNG METAL ATTACK

I WASN'T EXPECTING ANYTHING AND I wasn't looking for anything. I was just playing a tape against my will because I frowned on playing unapproved demos at the store during business hours. For some reason I put it on despite my unfounded rules. As soon as I heard it I was blown away. I was smitten. I remember the first thing I thought was that this was America's answer to the NWOBHM. At the time, America had nothing to compare to it. It was America's answer to Motorhead. I wanted to work with these guys and get involved with them, although I knew nothing on the subject of producing a band.

On the demo was a number to call, K.J. Daughton. I ran to the only payphone at the flea market with change from the drawer and called the number on the tape, leaving Marsha alone to look after the store. She saw me get all excited and focused instantly, always supporting my actions. We had spoken about how the music had blown me away and tried to figure out ways to contact the guys. I had some shows booked for Venom in the area and there were shows with Twisted Sister coming up that I thought Metallica would've been

Jon Zazula

great for. There were shows I wasn't even booking but knew I could get them on. What K.J. did was contact Metallica's drummer, Lars Ulrich, and had him contact me so we could talk. One night during dinner I received a phone call from Lars, followed by a letter from him introducing himself and the band to me. Right there on the phone we went straight to business. I told Lars about the bands we were working with and the shows we were promoting, all of which excited him, especially the upcoming Venom dates. He, being a student of the NWOBHM himself, felt his band was on the right path coming to the east coast for these shows. I spoke to their tour manager, Mark Whitaker, about bringing them across the states, agreeing on sending them $1,500.00 to drive over in a rented U-Haul and their pick-up truck. I used the money from that weekend's flea market earnings to fund this. The money was sent over through Western Union and I didn't even think about the financial risk of just sending money to some teenagers in California. Of course, that money was supposed to pay for merchandise for the next week, but I believed in them, so Marsha agreed and the money was sent. Marsha had a strong belief in me her whole life ... GOD knows why.

Here was the deal: they would come to the east coast and stay at my house. I had bands stay at my house a night or two before so it wasn't a big deal. These Metallica shows were during a 3-4-week period. When they arrived at the driveway of my house in the U-Haul truck like The Nina, The Pinta and the Santa Maria, they got out and the first thing they said to me was, "where's the booze?" I had a house full of company and the first thing Metallica did was say hello to everyone while they were eyeballing my liquor laid out on my wagon bar. They were fixated on my bar. After looking at it from the corners of their eyes, they dove straight in that direction, drinking it right from the bottles. My first impression of them was they were very young and had an "I don't care" attitude, very punk rock. More than that, I wondered what I had gotten my wife and I into.

We took them to the store that first day because they were really interested in seeing it and I felt my house was not the final stop of their visit. I wanted them to get out and see the flea market and get excited. We packed everything back up, they took a couple of bottles from the bar, and off we went. Their guitarist, Dave Mustaine, took a fifth of vodka with him, as an example of their alcohol intake which always seemed to amaze me. While we were away at work all day and worked on booking these shows, they would just hang out at the house. The thing that fascinated me with Metallica was they went to bed after me but they woke up at 5-6 in the afternoon. They were like vampires. It was uncanny and very different than the way Marsha and I lived. Soon, however, having this young band living in our house wasn't working out too well, with all the partying they were doing. There was a point where Raven, Venom and Metallica were all hanging at Casa Z! I was trying to work in a small area of the basement with my desk surrounded by sleeping bodies that were always snoring away. It was insane! After a while Marsha and I rarely went down to the basement because we were working on what was needed to get things rolling, or taking care of the children. We were constantly balancing two different worlds under the same roof. We were lucky the Old Bridge Militia, a group of metal fans who Metallica dubbed their name, would take them back to their place, feed them and keep them there to get them out of our heads for a couple of hours.

I sent them over to Ray Dill's house for a while and

then Anthrax stepped in to help out. Anthrax, at the time, were a heavy metal band out of Queens, NY, who kept pestering us with their almost—but quite not there—demos. We knew them well from the store and their uncanny ways of being backstage at every show. They suggested Metallica could stay at their rehearsal spot, The Music Building located in Jamaica, Queens, which was very nice of them. The Music Building was a big and old building that had every room occupied by a band. About 50 bands or so rehearsed there. When we got there, the owner of the studio told us Metallica could not sleep in the music rooms by law. The only area available he had was on the top floor where there was a storage space. It was horrible, shit everywhere, rats, broken wood and beds with springs coming out of them, dust, *yuck!* But that was the only area available for them and that's where they stayed. At this point I just gave Metallica money so they could barely eat. I felt I was certainly in over my head. Feeding my own family was still difficult and I didn't know all this responsibility was coming my way. At this point they were all my kids. All four of them. Every expense, every need for a bathroom, every need for a bed, food, strings, clothes, picks and when I couldn't even take care of my own mental health it became a big responsibility.

From the start you could feel a disconnection between Dave and the other members of the band. Dave would drink a lot and he would take on different personalities and you would never know which Dave you were getting. You bit your nails during the entire set never knowing what he was going to do, but I must admit he never let me down during the show, not for a single note. He always had it together musically. The other three guys would sort of ask me my opinion up and down a whole bunch of times about removing him from the band. I didn't see that they even had a choice in doing that.

They reassured me they had another guitarist lined up who would fit in like a glove and not to worry. Those guys made the transition arrangements to fire Dave and fly in their new member, Kirk Hammett. They took care of that situation themselves very fast. One day Dave was there, next day he was gone and Kirk arrived. They were on a mission and nothing was going to derail that mission.

By this time, Metal Joe, one of Old Bridge Militia founders, had moved Metallica to his house in Farmingdale, NJ. The band lived there in a much healthier environment than the horrible Music Building. Joe's home was dubbed the Fun House. It was one crazy time. Metallica not only performed live in Metal Joe's basement but they also wrote a good portion of what was to become *Ride the Lightning* there. In a short while Slayer hung out there and they played, too, down in the Fun House Basement for the militia and friends. There were no words to describe these times. The air was filled with madness.

When I first met Kirk he was a very quiet guy and I was worried he was too quiet for the insanity Metallica was, but he was a mean guitar player who fit in right away. Kirk got all the tracks down super quick and efficiently. It was smooth sailing for them. For Kirk's first performance we booked a show in Dover, NJ at the Showplace which used to be a strip club during the day and a rock club by night. We had a radio station out in Dover, WDHA, who had a midnight metal show that would promote the shows we booked in the area. From there we planned and booked shows across the New York tri-state area. Can you imagine: Metallica and Anthrax on the same stage New Year's Eve in Mount Vernon, NY playing to less than 150 people? Uncanny to think such a thing is possible, yet it's true. Those days were a building process and Metallica's live performances got better every time you saw them. Marsha and I found the audiences followed the shows from venue to venue and the attendance numbers kept increasing. It was the band constantly working the Northeast that built them a following of 500 fans who attended the historic Rio Theatre show in Long Island, NY the following year. It is my favorite Metallica show to this day.

Lars and I always discussed the idea or the possibility of doing an album. I even made a few phone calls to people in the business to put it out there, but no one in the business interested. nor was there interest in listening to their demo tapes, or seeing them live. They didn't get it. They just thought it was noise. Out of necessity to have this music out, Marsha and I talked constantly and I was able to convince her we should do it ourselves. I had zero clue on what it meant or what it took to release a record. My lack of knowledge cost me dearly in the beginning. People preyed on me like I was a chicken in a slaughter house. I was trusting their handshakes while their other hands had knives in my back. These were just the folk who I relied on. I was basically out there alone. The only guidance I had was from the divine voice that never stopped speaking to me, pushing me forward and giving me the answers, to whatever came my way, and Marsha who took all those words and made it clearer for me to understand. Together Marsha, my Divine Power, and myself decided to do it with faith in Metallica. We were ready to approach the band and tell them our plans. At that time the band were eager to record an album. They liked the idea of an all-metal record label, so we made an agreement to record some albums. There wasn't much more to it than that. You could feel something huge was in the making.

I wanted to call the label Vigilante Records because we were doing it ourselves, but the name never stuck.

One day I went to Times Square in NYC and saw a movie called *Vigilante* that was playing alongside another one called *Megaforce* which ended up being a box office disaster. I looked at that title and thought what a great name for a label! The Megaforce. I came up with the original logo of the two fists pressing against the Megaforce logo which I found out later meant "The Force" in sign language.

All of this was done with Marsha's support and her believing in me and the vision I had. We were not making any real money yet, despite the shows doing well. While the future looked bright by the time we all decided to go into the studio it became apparent what it costs to record an album the right way. Producers, engineers, 2"tape, ½" tape, catering, lodging and, oh boy, studio rentals just to get started. Then there was the search to find a producer who could capture Metallica's live sound, which proved very hard to do.

In my search for the proper studio I spoke to Joey DeMaio, the bass player for Manowar. He suggested a place in upstate New York, at the time called Barrett Alley. Joey told me the studio had a great sound and a great producer. I called the owner of the studio, Paul Curcio, and we spoke about doing the Metallica album. We agreed on working on it but then I told him I had no money and I'd have to pay him later. Surprisingly he was okay with this. He probably thought he'd get the money out of me one way or another. I was taking a huge financial risk here because I was going to pay him back with money we made on album sales, hoping we would make enough in return. Remember, I never shipped a record in my life. Unbelievably, I ended up paying the studio bill before I left with the finished tapes. Our record store earnings and a second home mortgage paid for the album. Curcio made it easy for me to pay him in installments, but raising the money for all the incidentals was killing us but we managed somehow to find the money to get through.

While we were recording, I wasn't with the band daily but I was with them a lot. I found a man named Ron Stein and his lovely wife Jackie from a local record store in Rochester, NY who owned Lakeshore Records. They took an interest in the band and helped take care of them and fed them while they were in the studio.

It took a long time for the sound to come together once they started recording. On one of my final visits, singer and rhythm guitarist James Hetfield came up to me very mad. He told me the producer said the record was over, the record was finished and that it sounded like an Allman Brothers or Santana record. It didn't sound like Metallica at all. There was no crunch to the riffs. I had a fight with the producer and the engineer who thought it was sounding great. James and I sat with them and listened to the album together making notes on the needed corrections to heavy up the entire record and to crunch up the sound. James hadn't even been allowed to come in and do his heavy rhythm guitar overdubs, so the sound was one dimensional. We had to fight to add in those needed tracks so at the end of the day you have what you hear now. Thankfully we got a great sound engineer in Chris Bubacz to mix the album properly, the way it was supposed to be. At that time there was no metal sound like Metallica's for the engineer to reference; Bubacz was in uncharted waters.

The album title they decided on, *Metal Up Your Ass*, was something I loved. In fact, I came up with the concept of the toilet bowl with the fist coming out of it with a sword. That was all ready to go until I was told by distribution at Important Records that retailers and buyers wouldn't carry it. I had to break the news to the band and they were pissed about it. Metallica's bassist Cliff Burton just said, "Man, fuck those big business guys, fuck the suits, we should just KILL EM ALL!" That was the Metallica way. It was a brilliant moment and we soon changed the name.

In the summer of 1983, Metallica's first album titled *"Kill 'Em All"* was released. I came up with the concept for the photo of the cover, hired a photographer and explained to him what we wanted. He shot it and the band really liked it. *Thank GOD!* That same photographer also took the iconic group photo, that I really love, seen on the back cover of the album. It captures just what type of record this was going to be. This wasn't a hair band. These teenagers in denim and leather, acne and all were here to deliver an album unheard of by an American band.

The record store was doing very well at that time and all sales from the store, instead of paying for more records at Important, or using it to pay our mortgage, every dime went to pay for *Kill 'Em All*. We were living broke. I don't know how we managed during that time. It was like a mental tornado, the damage that was being done to my mind coupled by the fact the workload many times demanded a 24-hour day.

After completing the recording, it was time to manufacture records to sell to the masses. The only problem was all of our finances were fully depleted. It's very important that I mention two instrumental people who helped Marsha and I at this pivotal time, Marsha's sister Hedy and brother-in-law Nat Tehrani believed in us from the very beginning and invested in us to get the *Kill Em All* album manufactured, which also got the label off the ground. Our first pressing was 5,000 units and went from there. The Tehrani family were also there to help produce The Halloween Headbangers Ball concert when no one else would even give us the time of day. Thank you, Hedy and Nat, for your support and belief which helped to make this story possible. We are forever grateful to you both.

Around this same time, we had Anthrax stalking Marsha and I everywhere we went. They were giving us demo after demo and we rejected them because they weren't good enough. The demos were interesting but we felt they needed more if they were to go into the studio. Their guitarist Scott Ian and bassist Danny Lilker were relentless, trying all the time to get our attention. Anthrax would constantly visit us at the flea market and they were truly a big nuisance, like, "Oh no, here they come again." I mean, they had an "Anthrax" license plate, the balls on those guys! One day I took my family out to IHOP to get breakfast and there was Scott with company following me from the parking lot of the restaurant. I told him not to bother me while I'm waiting in line with my family trying to eat like the rest of America. So, while I'm eating my breakfast, he gave me a new demo with the song "Soldiers of Metal" on it which was produced by Ross the Boss of Manowar fame. When I went home to listen to it I really loved it. They had passed the Zazula listening test. I thought they did a great job improving their sound and style. The recording sounded great! I gave them a record deal right on the spot. To introduce them to the world, Megaforce put out the 45" single of "Soldiers of Metal." We printed around 2,000 copies followed by the full-length album.

Things were starting to pick up and with Metallica's new album, signing Anthrax, setting up Venom and Manowar shows and taking care of our family it was a balancing act trying to figure out how to give ourselves equally to all people. I would start in the morning and end late at night, a simple routine. I barely slept during this period, at most a measly three hours a night. Metallica would be sleeping in the basement of our house while I would stay up working all day with their feet and bodies sprawled out all over the place. I don't know why I was so focused and hell bent on doing this. The only thing that I remember was the voice in my head which continually told me to move on. I honestly don't know what else to say. I was being told to do this so I followed and listened. It seemed the Lord was pushing me forward, constantly moving things ahead and never giving Marsha and I a chance to slow down.

CHAPTER 5

ROCK UNTIL YOU DROP

I WAS BOOKING SO MANY SHOWS during '83-'84 that some didn't actually happen. I was bringing Accept from Germany to the United States with an excellent band from the Netherlands, Bodine, to join Manowar in what was to be dubbed, "World War III." There was a guy who had contacted me from Europe telling me he was Accept's manager, bringing me great pictures of the band, shirts and merch. He was a great guy who stayed at my house for a little while and hung out at the store for the weekend. It turned out he wasn't their manager! I was getting sold a band that wasn't his and he was never in contact with them. It was a total hoax. Meanwhile, everybody was telling me I was talking to the wrong guy, which I didn't believe. So, the real manager of Accept came out after that situation and called me a liar, a crook, and that I was trying to steal the band from under her. There were all these claims and I thought everyone was insane, but they were right because the man staying in my home *was* an imposter. I laugh now at how absurd it was, this guy staying at my house while the entire time he wasn't even affiliated with the band. Since I had told everyone Accept was going to play and headline, we quickly switched the bill to Manowar as headliner with Virgin Steel and Cities to support making this an all "USA Power Metal" show.

Manowar's album on EMI records was something that caught my attention. I wanted to meet them and try to book them a show but no one would take my phone calls. So, I called Bill Aucoin's office, who was the former manager of KISS, who managed Manowar at the time. Without having a magazine of my own, the band's publicist, Ida Langsam, allowed me to do an interview with the band making it my first freelance composition. Now, here I am at Aucoin's office, pencil and pad in hand and into the room marches Manowar's guitarist, Ross the Boss. At first you could cut the air with a sword. Ross was in full Manowar head and attitude. I remember it taking me more than a while to build rapport . But once we did the conversation began to unfold the EMI story. Ross told me there was yet another Manowar album in the can and he and bassist Joey DeMaio were looking for a new record label for its release. The first thing I said to myself was, "Don't do it Jonny. Don't go there!" But then the other voice said, "Maybe we should do something together."

I told Ross what I had worked on and where my future plans were with Megaforce. As a result, there were further conversations with both Ross and DeMaio where I explained how Manowar can be part of this unstoppable movement, and they let me at it. Both Ross and Joey were great visionaries and our friendship grew fast. They liked me enough to allow us to book several shows and after a while trusted me to release their classic album, *Into Glory Ride*, on Megaforce in 1983. They were so serious about the Megaforce deal that they signed the record contract with their own blood. I am a witness. They slit themselves with a knife and filled the quills with blood. Of course I was asked to join in but I declined.

It seemed like a new batch of bands emerged quite quickly during this time and I had the opportunity to work with some real groundbreaking stuff. Mercyful Fate was this great band out of Denmark we were all crazy about: the sound, the vocals, the imagery, the musicians were all so creative and unique. Their singer King Diamond was a prolific vocalist with satanic face paint that really set a new standard for how a front-man could lead a heavy metal band. I cut a deal with the head of Roadrunner Records in Europe, Cees Wessels, since he wanted to bring Mercyful Fate to America. Megaforce became the label for their album "Melissa," and we broke them in America, giving them an audience within the broad reach we were building.

At the same time, I was listening to Raven's "Rock Until You Drop" album and saw a number on the back of it. I called, and David Wood, the head of their record label Neat Records, a small heavy metal label in Newcastle, England, picked up and we started talking about Venom and Raven. I was interested in booking shows and working with both bands but Raven primarily.

Neat Records licensed Raven's new album *All for One* to Megaforce. So, we worked with Raven on releasing the album and had them headline a summer tour with Metallica. I didn't know what to do with the bands so we felt a U.S. tour would be a great idea to reach new fans who hadn't heard of them before. Please understand it was not common for small indie labels to promote and pay for national tours. We called it the "Kill 'Em All For One Tour," a play on both of the bands' newly released albums. The only problem was no one wanted to book them. It was a dry Sahara with the phone calls we made. Not a single place wanted to work with us. These promoters just didn't get it. They didn't see the vision and future with the eyes I had. I knew this was something special, so through some higher power I was set to make it work. While I was in Upstate New York recording *Kill 'Em All* I met an agent in Buffalo, a young guy starting out named John Dittmar. Once it came time to book these shows he was the one who set it up for us with odds stacked against him, and he succeeded. So now I had the tour and the question was: *How do we get them from venue to venue?*

I then visited a man in Putnam County, in Upstate New York who had a good deal on a Winnebago. Renting one would be much cheaper than riding the bus or getting a van. We had no roadmap as to how something like this was done so we just always went with what came cheapest. I talked to the guy who owned it, rented it with my name on it and took out some insurance (I prayed I wasn't going to need it) and off Raven and Metallica drove into the sunset.

Some of the venues John booked were huge! Some of the shows in the Southwest were just a little too big for the bands to play in. John knew this, but the buyer of the shows sold us up and down about this huge following these bands had in his markets. When reality time came, shit hit the fan. We got in a lot of trouble for overselling the bands, the local promoters, who were overzealous, believed that these bands were big name rock star acts that would bring in 10,000 people, which was a massive overstatement. In Bald Knob, Arkansas, they played at a huge venue and only brought in maybe 100 people. Promoters were expecting us to pull in with trailer trucks and a big crew of workers with light shows. Boy were they pissed when a small Winnebago drove up with all the equipment in the back! We had to drive up to the nearest shop and get two forklifts to be able to hang lights ourselves because we had no trusses and riggers to hold them for the shows. I don't know if you can imagine that? Some places didn't even have a stage, yet they were huge and expected us to set-up our equipment and have our own production. In one instance the local promoter was so furious he had the local police escort us out of town.

Despite all of these missteps our first time around, the tour was a complete success. We sold a lot of band merchandise and people took notice. Raven and Metallica played an amazing show in Chicago which we filmed for them in case they would ever want to use it for a music video or promotion. I flew out to Chicago from New Jersey because I saw the bands developing in a huge way and wanted to film them early in their careers for all to see. The bands had something special live and I knew they put on magical performances night after night. Experiencing them live would always thrill me. I was always happy and at the same time, always worried they weren't going to pull it off, but they *always* did. They were magical bands in a very special time. Just look at that Chicago show, all that energy, all that madness. It was incredible. These performances just reinforced my belief that Metallica would definitely grow into, as I believed from the beginning, the next Led Zeppelin.

The Winnebago went through hardships and got beat up pretty badly going through small parking lots, tunnels and roads. Backlights were smashed from crashing into things they couldn't see. I would get phone calls from the boys on the road, "Whoops, sorry Jon, it's a mess, this broke and that broke." The guy who owned it would call me as well, asking about the shape of the Winnebago and I honestly didn't know how bad it was. Once the band reached California, the owner had a friend go to one of the concerts to check on his vehicle. The whole thing was a fucking wreck, broken, beat and done. That was the end of that Winnebago.

They had to leave it in California. Thankfully, we got that insurance, which covered the damages, otherwise there was no way we could've paid for it.

Though the Winnebago died, the tour was a success. Everybody loved them, I had no doubters in my circle. You saw Metallica and their live performance would take you to the top of the mountain. End of story. Raven at that time were fresh and exhilarating. Listen to a song like "Hard Ride" off their first album and you'll understand what I mean. That album was recorded for about 1,000 pounds with one take and one group of the greatest fucking musicians. You'll hear the greatest jam, grooves and change ups, I mean *genius* stuff. There's a song called "Hellraiser" on it, a cover and tribute to Sweet that literally kicks your ass. I always said Raven were my number two favorite band of all time, but who's really number one? I don't know. Is it the Jefferson Airplane? Cream? The Beatles? Although I never saw the Beatles live, I saw the others live many times and I can tell you I strongly believed these two bands, Raven and Metallica, would become bands of that caliber.

As 1983 came to an end we began working on the debut album of Anthrax. It was difficult to get studio time in return for a percentage of the album's sales. It was too much of a risk. I had little money and believe it or not managed to convinced some great fellow who owned a studio in Upstate New York, that was supposed to be really good, to let us record a good sounding album and not pay for it until the end. Carl Canedy, the album producer, put the deal together and when we arrived at the studio we found out it was somebody's house. It wasn't like a real studio at all. GOD, the embarrassment. We loaded up the truck for our month away to record and ended up at somebody's house after driving six hours to Upstate New York. We had no money for hotels or food, but we weren't going to quit. I knew getting there would always be tough and I had to lead them to success, but what was I supposed to do? The album would cost $8,000 and I lead the band to some guy's home studio in the winter. I called Carl to see if we could figure something out and he told me about an engineer who had a studio in Ithaca, New York, named Alex Perialis, who would later become the engineer and producer on many Megaforce projects. The very next day we made the drive to meet Alex and to our luck it was a real studio this time around. Once I got there everything was going fine until the money situation came up. With this new studio we didn't have the plan like we did to pay later and record now so I had to talk to the head of the studio, Alex's father. His father owned half of Ithaca, or I like to believe he did, anyway. Turns out, Alex's father, John Perialas, was in New York City on business, so we had to go there to meet with him, leaving the band and Carl at the studio to learn what the results would be. We met at some restaurant face to face and talked about my store and my vision. He spent a half hour telling me he doesn't run a charity and that it was a good studio. He told me he couldn't help me out so I asked the weekly cost of the studio. I figured I could pay weekly for it. After he told me how much it was per week I suggested I could pay him that amount starting after week two, and have it so it was paid in full before we left the studio; he agreed with a handshake. Here I was again making the right moves, taking the meetings I needed to in order for my vision to come true for these bands. I went through financial pain time and time again because I believed in these bands and I believed in what we were doing. This was the second time I shook someone's hand for a deal, the first being Paul Curcio on *Kill 'Em All* and now, John Perialas. Beautiful.

Once the album came out I was so surprised at the outcome because the band really became a band in the studio. They forged their sound and it was amazing standing there and hearing "Metal Thrashing Mad" for the first time recorded and mixed. Carl and the boys delivered a great sounding record for me and Megaforce was really proud to have it. Ultimately though at the end I was still six months behind in payments: I owed Important Distributors, I was six months behind on my mortgage, and at that time I was honestly just six months behind on everything in life. *Kill 'Em All* and the new Anthrax album, *Fistful of Metal,* is where all my money went instead of paying for my other responsibilities. These big deals were done on my character and the character of the people I met who believed in me and shook my hand. They saw my vision and joined me in making it come true. I look back at those deals I made and the money we used and think about the amount of time and dedication we gave these bands.

Megaforce's first six months should've bankrupted Marsha and I but we prevailed like we always did. We somehow managed to keep going.

CHAPTER 6

1984

WHEN THE FREEZING WINTER CAME in January of 1984, Metallica played some east coast dates on their own. There were about twelve shows in all, some were openers and some were headliners. On the last day of the shows in Boston, they were scheduled to play two shows at The Channel where a lot of punk bands played at the time. Before the band returned home, someone broke into Metallica's van and stole a bunch of equipment, almost everything. Part of the drum kit, Marshall amps with modified cabinets and speakers, merchandise and records were all taken. This was a horrible thing to happen, especially when there was no money to replace any of it. It was like getting shot with a bullet through the head or clubbed with a baseball bat. For me everything was a big deal and I always blew it out of proportion, but this moment was an extremely low point for us all. I was there to look after these young bands and I felt I hadn't done my job.

I agonized over this for a while and was sinking into a deep hole mentally, physically and financially. I felt there was no answer to this predicament and there were other shows on the horizon. Endorsements were hardly what they are today so there was no free gear for my bands and I didn't have a pot to piss in. Marsha kept up the strength and never folded. She helped me to see the light like she always did, so we got up and walked on. I prayed this would work out and the Lord would give me direction and help me find the answer to get our asses and the band's ass out of this jam. What else were we supposed to do *Dear Lord?* These are horrible things to go through but you have to learn from these experiences.

Metallica and I were making plans for the recording of a second album. In order to raise money to get Metallica started in Sweet Silence Studio in Denmark, we licensed the second album to a UK label who really knew their stuff called Music For Nations (MFN). Steve Mason owned MFN along with Martin Hooker and had booked Metallica with Venom overseas. These European shows would take place once the U.S. east coast leg was over, where Metallica finished up the dates using gear borrowed from Anthrax, Ray Dill and Metal Joe from the Old Bridge Militia .

When Metallica left for Europe to record their second album, *Ride the Lightning,* we lost a lot communication with the band. Phone costs were huge which prohibited me calling nearly as much as needed. During *Kill 'Em All* the band and I worked together daily, not on musical direction but on visions, goals and aspirations. Previously, I knew where they were at all times and communication was constant. That had faded by the second album. Then the money problems began. The daily per diems were extremely small based on our budget to record the album. In fact, the cost between what we had earned from U.S. sales and the advance given to us by our foreign licensor MFN would give us very little left for manufacturing, marketing, advertising, etc.

Since the band was in Europe and the bills were paid in non-U.S. currency, we had our licensee MFN pay all the bills directly rather than pay us and we pay the bills. Now this was a practical means of doing business in the world of licensing overseas. For instance, if the band was touring in Europe it would be the European licensee that would pay the bills for the touring, rather than the money coming to the states. I mention this because this caused a rift, I believe, between Metallica and Megaforce. It seemed like every time we needed money, Megaforce would turn to MFN with its hands out. In truth, however, we were so tight back home running the company that we were fortunate to have MFN at the time. But the band believed the money coming out of MFN was not really my money and that MFN was now calling the shots.

I visited England once during that time and met up with James to hear some of the tracks from the *Ride the Lightning* session. I was a little blown away that after 100 hours of recording it was just drum tracks and some bass. It was obvious things were not as they had been back home. Maybe, it occurred to me, things may have been very different if I had been able to spend more time in Europe and bond with the band rather than running Megaforce and trying to develop the label back home.

I was in over my head from the day I started so I became easy prey for the vultures of the industry who tried to make a quick buck. Those with experience benefitted from my inexperience because they were making a living out of this for a long time and knew every trick of the trade.

I wasn't involved this time around with the album and I felt separated from the band. I was never shown any demos or rough mixes. The final and finished product was the first time I heard it. This album had an elevated sound from the first one, the production and drums mixed were quite an improvement from their previous endeavor.

When they came back from Europe it was instantly apparent that the connection we had, the vibe we had, was all gone. The companionship we had built was destroyed. They now had their own agenda. Where once they would look up to me to make the decisions, now they were within themselves in their own frame. Our bond wasn't the same and there was something different in the air when we all got back together. I no longer held that spiritual guide vibe anymore. I had lost it. All I could do was try my hardest to hold this mass of energy called Metallica together. Megaforce was still looking for distributors or a major label to pick up Metallica. We needed help with the first album's sales that were overwhelming for our small staffed label and promote the band as much as humanly possible. I was worried about Manowar, worried about Anthrax, worried about Metallica, but never had the time to worry about my mental health. My mental health would always come last since I worked day and night for these bands. I was on a mission and my mind was focused everywhere on everything. I have Marsha to thank for the amount of fortitude she showed during these times where I was about to lose every brain cell I had left. Marsha would talk to me as I walked around with my hands over my head talking to myself with the overwhelming emotion of stress and her voice alone would calm me down. She has a way about her to be able to reach me unlike any other and it was the divine pushing and prodding I felt from above that had me take on so much at one time. I realized that the power and the strength of a label and its artists depends on the ever-flowing money from sales of new product generated in a timely manner, and this on top of everything else, had to be done so no band suffered from lack of marketing promo, press, touring, etc.

After the Megaforce Roseland Showcase in August of '84 we were left without a singer for Anthrax to continue on with. There was a guy named Matt Fallon who sung for them for a little while but the vibe just wasn't there and his tenure didn't last very long so the search continued.

Around that same time I was having trouble finding some acts that were fresh and new. We decided to minimize the risk and cost of putting out four E.P's by working on a compilation of four bands on one record doing 2-3 songs each. So, *Born to Metalize* was created. It featured music from Tortured Dog, Sneak Attack, Hades and The Beast. These were local bands from the Tri-State area and I thought we could get buzz on any one of them and go from there in developing their careers. The record was released but was not a success in comparison to what else was happening on the label at that time.

Also in development was T.T. Quick, a New Jersey band who played on the local club scene. Their guitarist David DiPietro was Zakk Wylde's guitar teacher and the band, which started off as an AC/DC cover band, had a lead singer, Mark Tornillo, who made you believe Bon Scott was in the room performing. Today, Mark sings for both Accept and T.T Quick. Marsha and I felt someone should take a chance on them and since I loved their original material, so we decided to put out their album on Megaforce as well. They weren't the thrash metal type of band I was working with so I started a side label called Avalanche which would be for hard-rock bands, but that never worked out. Unfortunately, TT Quick were crushed under the rocks. What came out of this time in Megaforce history was a recording session with the acclaimed producer Michael Wagener that gave us one hell of a gem of a five song E.P. that stands the test of time. The E.P. didn't succeed on Megaforce/ Avalanche records as hoped because our label didn't have the finances and the power to bring TT Quick to radio where they belonged. We had decided to bring the band to Island Records, where we were having some success with Anthrax. However, as the TT Quick project was ready for release, the president of Island Records was replaced and the new regime weren't fans. One half of the album was produced by Michael Wagener and the other half by the world-famous Eddie Kramer, who had produced KISS and Jimi Hendrix, amongst other legendary artists. This was a combination that was unheard of. Unfortunately, the president of Island had just come over from Elektra and all he wanted from me was another Thrash band. He actually disliked the record so much; the album never had a chance to circulate. There was no radio or retail promotion, or any of the elements needed to break this band and we had to watch a great album go to waste.

As if this wasn't enough, while up in the studio in Rochester I decided, from a message from above, to record the first heavy metal rap song ever. "Metal Rap" came to me as a clear message. I resisted at first. How stupid of an idea this was? Yet the voices continued and when Carl Cannedy told me he would get the Rods to back me up I crossed the line and recorded the song. The song lyrics were not even written at this time. It was simply said to me, "Go do it." I went to the liquor store, bought a bottle of Jack Daniels, and out came the lyrics. I called myself, "The Lone Rager." I often felt like that character fighting the battle for Heavy Metal. For the album cover I wore a sheet over my head and leather studs and belts around me ... GOD I was sweating like a pig underneath all that. I was honestly out of my mind by this point, completely mentally exhausted and heavily into drugs to keep me going. The words just poured out and I always hoped someone would take the time to listen to them. They really depicted the status of Heavy Metal in the world at that moment. *"What's that loud brash noise I hear that leaves a ringing in my ear? Makes plaster fall and foundations resettle; oh my god it's HEAVY METAL!"* It was also fun recording the song because I got to involve my daughter Rikki and a few of her friends as background singers. My experience with Rap music was pretty much limited at that time to Public Enemy, Run-DMC and LL Cool J. To this day I don't know why I gave in and recorded "Metal Rap."

Then the voices in my head were louder than ever. I don't know where this came from, but on top of everything I had another dream that was absolutely INSANE. I sat up in my bed at 4 o'clock in the morning with an entire plan and song list of a band that HAD to be on Megaforce Records. My main focus was to work with iconic psychedelic band Blue Cheer and my goal was met that same year through the powers that be. Unfortunately, I forgot a lot of the tales that went into the making of *The Beast Is Back*. I never thought we would get through the recording of this record alive. We had the original drummer Paul Whaley and singer-songwriter and bass player Dickie Peterson in this historic line-up. One thing I must tell you is that Carl Cannedy produced this record and did an amazing job with the patience of a saint. *The Beast Is Back* remains one of the most enjoyable collections of music that I still listen to today. It truly was a miracle this album was ever completed.

Those days were totally insane. Bands were staying at our house after shows and in-between tours while we had recording sessions going on. It got so out of hand that Marsha and I received a letter from the community of Old Bridge stating we were running a boarding house because of all the people staying with us. They wanted us to stop this activity or legal actions would be taken. In true Z-style, instead of cowering from this, the letter became the inner sleeve of our compilation album *From the Megavault.* We were treading on water but that was the way we responded to the threat. This compilation was mainly used to show exposure on Megaforce artist with songs not featured on their records, such as exclusive songs or B-sides. There was this band I really loved, Medieval Steel, from Memphis, Tennessee that didn't have enough material for an album, so they have a track on this album. Overkill and the rest of the Megaforce Family all had non-LP tracks so this is where they were assembled for public consumption. The one band you maybe never heard of was this really cool band Imperious Rex whose lead guitarist ran a management company out of the Pyramid Sound Studios. I enjoyed his band a lot and gave them a track on the album as well, hoping more would come out of it than it did. And if all of this going on in the relatively short period of time wasn't enough, the new Megaforce home for recording moved officially from Rochester to Ithaca making Pyramid Studios their new home.

1984 proved itself to be even crazier by us putting Exciter into the studio to release their epic Megaforce album, *Violence and Force.* While Exciter were in the studio, I remember I was going through highs and lows almost simultaneously in my mind and I started to doubt my ears for the first time. I had a hard time during this recording session and believed my relationship with the band was not as wonderful and warm as some of the other artist we had worked with. Exciter would never go on to be a permanent member of the Megaforce Family and we would release just one album; Later on, we did end up releasing their first album, *Heavy Metal Maniac,* along with *Violence & Force* as a special double-package.

If this all didn't seem like enough, in 1984, things were in a frenzy at our Rock n' Roll Heaven booth at the Rt. 18 Flea Market. The building was sold and the new owners wanted us to move our location to some horrible corner in the back of the market. Marsha and I were not into this move so we decided to take the plunge and open a real brick and mortar record store somewhere in our beloved New Jersey. It had to be in close proximity to Old Bridge so we chose a town called Clark to be our new home. We were way too busy at the time to be at the store, which was now open six days a week instead of three. Our longtime friend, and part time manager, at the Flea Market was Brian Nyers. We asked if he would run our Clark store and he kindly accepted. One thing you should know about Mr. Nyers, he was a passionate salesman. If he wanted you to own an album he would tell you everything you could ever know about that vinyl. Rat Skates (Overkill's original drummer) gave him the nickname Brian "Buy or Die" Nyers. A great treasure at Rock n Roll Heaven was Brian's "Bathroom of Fame." All the bands who came to the store had to write on the bathroom wall; Slayer, Anthrax, and Overkill were just a few of our signatures. A few years later, due to the heavy work load at Megaforce and Crazed, we ended up closing the store and asked Brian to once again join the forces at the castle.

Throughout my book you will hear me talk about "highs and lows" but what you have to realize is this was a time before the use of Psychopharmaceuticals and my mind was racing in both directions. I was also constantly exhausted from the unholy hours that I kept. If I slept three hours a night, it was a miracle. I found myself using whatever drugs I could get my hands on to keep my work, family and financial life together. It would be much later on in life when I learned the words Bipolar and Manic Depression applied to me. This was just part of the madness that we loved to call 1984.

CHAPTER 7

SPEAK METAL OR DIE

W HEN ANTHRAX GOT READY TO record their follow up
to *Fistful of Metal* I was involved with them pretty
much every step of the way. If I didn't like a song
or lyric I would tell them, always trying to put in my
two cents, trying to keep them on the right track. They
didn't always agree with me but we had a positive
friendship that focused on one goal: To make a great
album. Once I arrived at the studio in Ithaca, the band
already had their new singer, Joey Belladonna. They
auditioned him in the studio and right away knew his
vocals were perfect for the band. Anthrax immediately
told me about his background and his amazing vocal
range but Joey didn't have a clue about Anthrax's style
of heavy metal. It was funny and it's true that I spent
hours during the sessions with Joey, singing him the
melody lines to songs on the album hoping he would
mimic my singing. I was so humbled when Joey sang
back to me what I was praying it would sound like.
When he and I got together at the Goodbye Slayer Fest
in 2018, the first thing Joey brought up was how funny
I was trying to teach him how to sing.

We had gotten to a point with the band that as

their managers we worked on every show, the setting, stage, lighting. We were as involved as possible with everything. It was really nice. The band was very warm and always made Marsha and I feel like a sixth member. They even let me write the lyrics to "Medusa" since they trusted me so much. When the album "Spreading the Disease" was finished, Megaforce decided to promote it with a music video for their lead single "Madhouse." We at the Zazula's wanted to shoot a high-end, 1980's MTV style music video, but it just wasn't going to happen. Sonically and visually, Anthrax's metal sound was the opposite of what MTV and the radio were playing. There was no point of attempting to go and pretend to be what they weren't. We shot the video at an abandoned mental institution with a bunch of loose patients moshing around to Anthrax's music. MTV flat out didn't want to play it. They thought it was too depressing and as predicted, sonically abrasive. Later on when the MTV show "Headbanger's Ball" came out "Madhouse" was played pretty extensively.

These were early days, and in the Madhouse video you can see the beginning of the popularization of moshing. The band wanted to promote not only the music but also the scene behind it, so the mosh pits became important in the videos. These Anthrax shows would get pretty fucking wild and the New York crowds would sometimes get out of hand, but they always wanted to capture that aspect in their music videos way before moshing became a mainstay at metal shows. Moshing had taken its own form throughout the club years in the city and that early phase was created during the NY Hardcore scene. CGBG's birthed that attitude and Anthrax adopted it from their love of punk and hardcore.

When *Spreading The Disease* was finished we actually had some extra studio time to kill, so I asked if the band had any extra material they'd like to record. Scott and Anthrax drummer Charlie Benante had actually been wanting to start a hardcore punk style thrash band with Danny Lilker who was now playing with Nuclear Assault, and their friend from the NY Hardcore scene, Billy Milano, which they were going to call Stormtroopers of Death, or S.O.D. for short. Marsha had heard some of the stuff they were jamming on and thought it was astonishing and brought it to my attention. I listened to it and thought, *"Holy shit this is great!"* But of course, without any money, I asked producer Alex Perialas if he could work on this with our shoestring budget of under $3,000. Now I needed this to be written, recorded, mastered, mixed and finished (with artwork) and done in just a few days ... and they did it. Billy got a friend of his from upstate New York to make the now iconic album cover and they wrote such a classic album, hit after hit. The band could've been huge but with the success of Anthrax, S.O.D hardly had any time to play enough live shows after the album came out. S.O.D birthed another new style of music combining their love for heavy metal guitars and punk vocals. I had been to CB's a few times to see punk bands but I never really fell into the crowd. However, I sure loved S.O.D. So many bands ripped off their style from day one and S.O.D became the forefront spark in the genre that crossed Hardcore and Metal.

Overkill, like Anthrax, were metal ragers from the Northeastern USA. From '83 we sold Overkill tapes at our store. They sold very well and you could hear their growth with every new cassette. Overkill came to Rock n Roll Heaven a lot and eventually Marsha and I took a shining to them. When they asked us to listen to their latest release on Azra Records we felt the band sounded great and unique enough to join the Mega-family. So Marsha called Pyramid Studios and made the arrangements for what was to be the final Megaforce release prior to our dealings with the major labels, which was right around the corner. When the band went off to shoot the album cover for "Feel the Fire," I told them make sure to use a raging fire. They almost burned down the entire area where the photo shoot took place and I remember the flames were so fierce that everyone in Overkill had smoking behinds when they got back to the studio. What was great about Overkill is they always delivered great albums to us. We were very proud to release "Feel the Fire" on October 15th, 1985, and we received a very good response making everyone at the label excited. We were joyous that we got it right again.

Sometime in 1985 Megaforce made a monumental production deal with Island Records for Anthrax. We at Megaforce would produce the albums, get a little override from the company and the band would get the rest. Island Records would distribute the albums worldwide and give the band and Megaforce their percentage.

The way we signed Anthrax to Island was a little strange. Chris Blackwell, owner of Island Records, invited me to his apartment in Manhattan at the Essex House. Once I got there I waited a while and when he joined me in the living room it was funny because he asked me, "So, do you have something for me, Jonny?" I talked to him about Anthrax and he asked me to put the tape on his player. When I played him "Armed and Dangerous," he came over to me and said, "Jonny is this the real thing? I only want the real thing." I felt that I was doing a drug deal and Anthrax was signed the following week.

Now we were working alongside the major leagues, cutting deals with worldwide distribution to get these bands in every store we could. Island and Megaforce decided to do this deal on a one by one basis where

Island would not be entitled to put out anything unless it was mutually agreed upon by both labels. Unfortunately, nothing materialized and it seemed this Island relationship was not going beyond Anthrax.

However, this deal with Island gave Anthrax the credibility needed to get them the direct support slot with Black Sabbath. They only received 6 shows but we made it sound like they've been Sabbath's support band forever. There was a considerable amount of touring to support that album in the United States. Island Records was also strong in the UK and Europe. The head of Island Records International, Phil Cooper, took a liking to Marsha and 1 and thank GOD he took us seriously and became a major player in the success Anthrax had overseas.

Because of the positive press the band received in the states and in Europe, the band grew in popularity, and notoriety immensely. The press wrote about the band through magazines like Kerrang!, Metal Hammer and Aardshok which were now getting popular in Metal Record stores and were starting to pop up everywhere. This also lead to further touring and brought the band to a great agent, Jeff Rowland, who was at the powerhouse agency ICM. Everything was getting serious and Anthrax was now in place. All the elements were there. All that was left was to find a brilliant agent for them overseas. In the meantime, I was talking to Chris Blackwell as Anthrax developed into a band to be contended with. We had taken our relationship into publishing and were getting more and more entrenched in Island. In the conversations we had, we were asked if we had another band to bring to the Island family but we already committed ourselves to a new suitor in the wings, Atlantic Records, and Overkill had been released in October of that year on Megaforce. This was the time when TT Quick was signed to Island while we were making a commitment to Atlantic. The reason we didn't take TT Quick over to Atlantic was because the current regime at Island was asking for a more hard-rock oriented record while Atlantic Records only wanted Megaforce Records to bring them their signature thrash sound. This was not the best situation for TT Quick as there was a regime change at Island Records. This was one of the first tragedies to befall our label in a very long time and did more harm to me and the band than is describable.

Megaforce and Crazed Management were starting to be taken quite seriously at this time worldwide. The success of Metallica and our other endeavors were starting to bear fruit. I don't know if we closed the store at this time but things were starting to look really good economically. However, we wanted to play with the big boys and bring the metal scene to the Major Leagues. So we entertained meetings with the major labels to become part of their world and see if that could escalate the marketing, growth and success of the Metal movement.

CHAPTER 8

THE TRIO OF STEEL

W E WERE ENDING OUR DEAL with Important Records as my distributor and I needed a new place to go. We didn't renew as we kept looking for a new family to distribute our product as an independent record company. This was for the records we had distributed through IRD to make sure they could continue to be released independently at the same time as we developed our larger acts through a major label.

We also realized there were certain bands that would have to start in the independent arena and not be brought into the big leagues until they had a buzz big enough for the majors to accept them no matter what kind of band they were musically. For independent distribution, Marsha and I decided to go with Caroline who were owned by Virgin Records at the time. Caroline got my interest because of the man who ran their distribution by the name of Keith Wood. His signing of the Misfits made me feel that I would be in good company. So Caroline became our independent distributor and remained so for years to come.

We now had two players in the room; Caroline for our independent and edgier stuff and Island Records for Anthrax and their product. There was one more player that we needed because Island only committed to the bands they wanted and we didn't want to argue when we came to a major label with a band. Atlantic Records and Crazed Management had a relationship with a gentleman by the name of Larry Yasgar. He was responsible for signing C+C Music Factory and Debbie Gibson to Atlantic Records amongst others. Larry was a smiling face, sarcastic kind of guy with a great sense of humor and always let you know he wasn't born yesterday. He saw the coming of metal and saw that Metallica was on Elektra, Anthrax on Island and they were starting to blow up. He's the person who signed Raven to Atlantic but wanted the whole ball of wax which was Marsha and me. Larry introduced me to the president of Atlantic Records, Doug Morris. We soon met with his staff for several hours and discussed our vision. It was apparent they were gambling on me and my ears and knew very little of the bands I represented. Surprisingly, the contract for Megaforce to become part of Atlantic Records came in just one day. It wasn't the greatest contract in the world but it promised me that Atlantic Records would fund the label with a fair budget, release five projects a year and distribute overhead for marketing to the company as well. Within a week we were signed, sealed and delivered and our quest with Atlantic had begun. That's how we got the trio of Steel; Atlantic for our big boys, Caroline for our independent and Island for our one off's and special situations.

Once all three distribution companies were set up it was time to figure out where we would place the artists that were lined up for the label. Even though Megaforce had Raven's catalog of "All For One" and "Live At The Inferno," Atlantic would not let us get involved with Raven in this deal. The groups we were bringing to the table were TT Quick, Overkill and M.O.D, with only

Overkill making it to Atlantic from the original Megaforce family. M.O.D came together from S.O.D's Billy Milano when it seemed apparent the other members of Anthrax were never going let S.O.D live a natural life. S.O.D, for a while, were competing with Anthrax and Metallica for the coolest band in the States. People were really flipping for S.O.D and the sound of it was amazing with "Chromatic Death" later being used as the theme song for Headbangers Ball on MTV without ever paying anyone a dime for it.

There were magazines in Europe and the U.K that would publish my Rock n Roll Heaven playlist. Everybody saw these playlists and they were extremely hip and accurate. The chart was based solely on the chart of sales from the store in New Jersey. Through these lists I became friends with some of the magazine writers in Europe who would call me and ask questions about the bands on my lists. These same writers became big influences in the metal scenes of their countries where their magazines were in print; Geoff Barton and Xavier Russell from KERRANG!, Ollie Klemm from Metal Hammer, Jurgen Wiggenhaus, owner of Metal Hammer in Germany and Metal Mike Rijswijk from Holland's Aardshock were amongst the press who I called friends in those days. I took the press so seriously in Europe that on the very first chance I had I went overseas and met them whenever and wherever I could've. Metal Hammer had expanded throughout Europe and I convinced the magazine to sponsor an all American tour throughout that region and they agreed. We named it "The U.S Speed Metal Attack" which was fitting for the U.S steel imported across the seas. The bands chosen by Metal Hammer were Anthrax, Overkill and Agent Steel. This tour lead the way for many of the American tours that followed for years to come. To sum things up, it was a huge success and all three bands were established from it in those territories, especially Anthrax.

THE LEGACY

During that summer we had an employee who was a dear friend of ours for many years named Maria Ferrero who took over the press at Megaforce and had a very strong hand in the A&R'ing of the label. One of the bands who approached her was out of the Bay Area called The Legacy. The band at that time featured singer Steve "Zetro" Souza, who in the middle of Maria presenting the band to me, left The Legacy for another project. I truly believe I gave Maria a super hard time about bringing this band into Megaforce. I felt they sounded too much like Metallica and I really just didn't get it. You have to remember in the early stages of a band they don't sound as good as they do when they get out of the studio and this is where The Legacy was at. For me, they weren't right for us, especially when they lost their singer. Maria never let up for a second and kept me aware of every breath of air the band took. There was a big change up for The Legacy and that was when they got new vocalist Chuck Billy and re-recorded their demo with Chuck's voice. I still wasn't completely sold on the band and didn't get a chance to see them live because I was flying out to Europe to see Anthrax who were touring with Metallica. It was set that once I returned from Europe I would go see The Legacy perform live at their rehearsal space In Oakland before I made my final decision.

It was very weird for me in Europe because I hadn't seen Metallica since we parted company. I felt the same way I did at the Roseland Ballroom all over again, that I was unwelcomed, so I just hung with Anthrax and it was business as usual. When you're a manager you want to get the experience of the whole thing so that you don't miss a beat with your band, so you can all be on the same pulse. I was also there to make sure everyone was being treated right. You never had to monitor Anthrax, you just got in the groove and went along with them. It was especially nice while I was over there because I did get to spend some quality time with Cliff Burton who was extremely cordial. Cliff was a total sweetheart to me during my visit and acted as if I had never left. He was a great guy and didn't give a shit about drama. We hung out and shared some mother nature together. The shows were a huge success. The new Metal Scene was about to start happening in a big way. The whole vibe was bigger than before and everybody was playing great together.

After our visit to Europe Marsha and I headed home to pick up our daughter Rikki and grab the next flight to San Francisco where we would meet up with The Legacy. The first night we were at our hotel we received a phone call at 3am from our partner Tony Incigeri,who remained in Europe on tour with Anthrax and he asked if I was sitting down. I asked, "Why are you calling me? It better be something serious." "Cliff is dead," he said. I thought he was fucking kidding me. He proceeded to give me the details that were available at that early time about Metallica's bus accident in Europe which claimed Cliff's life. Of course Marsha and I were in a state of shock. We were staying at some hotel and we quickly got dressed and took a walk down the long waterfront by pier 35 and walked and walked until daylight.

That night it was time to see The Legacy in their rehearsal space. We were still in shock from the news about Cliff. The space looked like the Music Building in New York, decrepit and filled with musicians in every available room. Every band in The Bay Area were there that night in their rental spaces and echoing behind every doorway of every studio you could hear a bass player playing Cliff's solo off of "Anesthesia Pulling Teeth." Marsha and I both said how our skin was crawling and by the time we saw The Legacy we were so fucking uptight. It wasn't even 24 hours yet and already this was going on, people looking to replace Cliff.

Down the hall, The Legacy opened the door and asked us if we were ready. Then they went and blew our fucking heads off. What happened for me was that Maria pushed them on me with such enthusiasm and vigor but I just didn't seem to connect to the songs as I did when I saw it live. It was what she was feeling the whole time and Marsha looked at me and gave me a smile and said, "Don't worry, we're gonna do this, Jonny." This was also the best of my memory of how this all happened. It was our decision to sign them—they left us no other option. We got hit by a bolt of lightning that this group was going to be something spectacular.

COMPASS POINT NASSAU BAHAMAS

Scott Ian wanted to record the next Anthrax album in the Bahamas like Iron Maiden did and it was my job to make his dream come true. They started writing and recording in the studio and the songs came out great. They had a little rehearsal space that I visited once a week in Yonkers, NY, and it was apparent they had some really brilliant material. We used to always watch what Iron Maiden was doing and saw a photo spread with them romping around some beautiful tropical island. It looked so wonderful that the band had just enough money in their recording budget to record their next record in Compass Point Studio which was owned and operated by Chris Blackwell. I spoke to Chris about taking Anthrax to the next level, and that we should really take a junket of people to the Caribbean where they could see Anthrax record their new album at his studio. We incorporated the band's album budget with their budget allocated to them for press worldwide and decided we would invite the most influential magazines of each territory down to the Bahamas and introduce them to both Anthrax and their new album, "Among The Living." Island agreed to it and this was our way to finally get major features needed to break Anthrax worldwide. The best part of the deal was the allotment of money Island gave me to personally supervise the project while they were in Nassau. The producer chosen for the album was Eddie Kramer and both Megaforce and Island were confident this was going to be a winner.

So Anthrax and management made their way to the Bahamas. The band had two three-bedroom houses and we were next door with our town house where we would live for the entire recording process. Thankfully the sessions went well and we had rough mixes early enough to have music for the press to get an early listen. I can't recall, but I believe we even brought down a photographer to do sessions in and around the island to furnish the press with photos. In the early development of the record you could see how Joey Belladonna was evolving more and more into an actual band member. The person who did the Among The Living album cover also did Metallica's Master of Puppets album cover, Don Brautigam, which was inspired by Stephen King's novel The Stand.

When the album was ready for release I went to Europe with Marsha and met with the press once again and the heads of all the Island Records affiliates to set up the band's return to Europe to tour this album. Among the Living came out both in the United States and Europe with a very successful amount of records sold, charting at #62 on the Billboard 200.

I remember *Spreading The Disease* went from 60,000 to more than 120,000 sales just on the back on the sales from *Among The Living*. This was proof I was correct that Island did not ship enough product on the release of *Spreading The Disease*. Thank GOD for Bill Berger and Rick Bleiweitz, who believed in me and the band enough to press as much product to cover the sales expectations of the album. It was like we had a dream team established with Island Records and *Among The Living* would eventually go Gold. We convinced Headbangers Ball on MTV to promote a national tour across America. Headlining was Anthrax, with Helloween and Exodus as support. I always believed Anthrax was smarter than me when it came to their attachment to their audience. I would never interfere and always green lit anything they gave me. It was a real stretch of faith when the *I'm The Man* E.P was released in 1987 after the release of *Among The Living*. I felt they were going way out on a limb and also felt this could destroy them, but the band wanted to take a chance and it was what they were into. They dug The Beastie Boys, Run DMC, Public Enemy and anything rap. They wanted to release the *I'm the Man* E.P and we honored their wishes by doing so. It was a very off to the left thing and it would either get attention and do good or get attention and do bad. I was very afraid of making a mistake in their career. I once made a mistake before by straying too far and dreaded another backlash.

It was a Godsend when the press in Europe made such a big deal over their rap E.P. They loved it or they were intrigued by it but nobody hated it, thank GOD! When Anthrax went to the U.K it became a welcomed part of their live show. From what I recall the U.K and European audiences were also intrigued by Scott Ian's popularization of the word "NOT." The use of "NOT" got so huge that the band developed a mascot, the "NOT MAN."

THE LEGEND OF THE NOT MAN

At Island Records, an advertising rep was asked to do a campaign on Anthrax as a teaser for the release of *Spreading The Disease*. He took a rubber doll face, stretched it out, took a photo of it and put it on a cover of an ad. On the top of the ad was the "Anthrax" logo, and underneath it said "It Works For Me." I hated it and wanted to know what it had to do with Anthrax. In fact, I was too embarrassed to show it to the band. It was so non-metal. The ad campaign ran without my approval and caused a brief war between Megaforce and Island. A week later people were talking about that campaign ad Anthrax had in the U.K and European magazines and wanted to know what it symbolized. Somebody in the press wanted to know if it was tied into the word "NOT" and I don't know if it was me, Scott Ian, Charlie Benante or this writer, but all of a sudden Anthrax had a mascot (unwillingly) who seemed to take on the name "The NOT MAN." By the time Anthrax got to Europe the merchandising company Bravado had developed a whole line of artwork of "NOT MAN" designs. From this point on he became a staple of those times. In the Anthrax video, "Antisocial," you could see Ozzy Osbourne wearing "The NOT MAN" head at the end.

Things were getting bigger and our organization had to expand. One of my weaknesses was that I had little road experience. Although I can help design sets and lighting I have no idea where you go to get these from. Most of my time was spent on the creative front of things. I was either in meetings, the office, or some recording studio. There was not enough time in the day to manage affairs both on the road and at the MegaKingdom, plus it was always imperative for Marsha and I to raise our children as normally as we could.

To handle production and manage the bands on the road I needed help and three names remain with me today. First and foremost, there was Mr. Anthony Incigeri, who became a dear friend and early partner. We first met when Tony booked bands at a great club in Brooklyn called the Brooklyn Zoo where he brought Raven's first show in the US. Whenever I needed a production question answered I'd call Tony. One night at the Paramount Theatre, Venom was live on stage and their sound started to rapidly change. I hadn't a clue why and they were sounding worse by the minute. Tony quickly pointed to the 12 Massive Perkins Bins on stage. He said, laughing, "See those black dots? That's them blowing out!" Eventually there was no bass sound coming from Cronos. He started going berserk until Tony explained that we all could still hear the bass guitar through the PA throughout the D I Channel on the board. The show miraculously went on. Right then on the spot I asked Tony to come on board and we became close partners.

Now with Tony on board, we made plans to take our shows on the road. From here on our bands could be showcased through the USA and with Tony there would be the knowledge to do this. Unfortunately, in time Tony and I grew apart, but together we made many historic inroads and I cherish those times. After Tony I worked with several Tour/Production people but it wasn't until I met Rick Downey when things started to move again. He was quite a Renaissance Man. I've met a few of these genius types in my life and Rick was a classic specimen. First off, Rick played drums for Blue Oyster Cult for a while and he tour managed

Motley Crue. More importantly he was a great lighting designer and he really took Anthrax to a whole new level. Rick was able to visualize all of our ideas for staging design and create it without fault. My favorite lighting design was his star curtain with moving clocks and giant Anthrax logo. Rick lasted as long as I was the manager of the band. We both left Anthrax within a short time of each other.

Then there was the *The Roadie of Death.*

While I'm talking about those who were responsible for keeping our bands on the road, my story would be incomplete if I didn't talk about our "Roadie of Death," Mr. Art Ring. Art was a college graduate who, when offered a job at a firm or to go on the road as a tour manager for William Burroughs, he chose life on the road. Art describes it all as, "I took the wrong fork in the road but ended up in the right place." At a hardcore Sunday matinee at CBGB's, Scott Ian saw this crazy stage tech running around for Suicidal Tendencies. Danny Spitz, Anthrax's other guitarist, needed a tech and Scott introduced them. It was very important to Dan that his tech specialized in Floyd Rose. When Dan asked Art if he knew Floyd Rose, Art replied, "I know him very well, he's one hell of a guy!" Somehow he got the job and Art stayed on with Anthrax for 5 years, moving on from us to be the stage manager for Ministry on the 1992 Lollapalooza Fest. In the final years of Megaforce and Crazed, Art stayed with us and was responsible for all touring of our bands throughout the world.

On the Megaforce front we had a press department run by Maria Ferrero, a radio promotion department run by Missi Collazzo and Jessica Harley. John Warden ran the video department while Gary Waldman ran retail. Brian Nyers, from Rock n Roll Heaven, ran the shipping department. There were 22 employees at Mega-Crazed. The accounting department had 4 people. Gabrielle

Incigeri ran the operation while Ed Trunk became the label Vice President. We had personal assistants. Some of our assistants had assistants. We had 10,000 square feet of office space. It was expensive but worth it. We sold records and were now in place to accommodate Atlantic and Island Records while running our Indie bands through Caroline.

Somehow through all of this, Marsha and I continued to raise a family and we made it our business never to miss a school function. We attended every school play and made it to every meeting with the teachers. I don't know where I found the energy or time to do so but there I was pulling 25 hour days, touring the world, raising a family and never missing a single beat along the way.

The Amazing Zazulas
My first band - 1963

1236 Burke Ave
The Projects

Me at 16 after a haircut

At 21 in Colorado

Rt. 18 Indoor Market
Photo Courtesy Fritch Clark

Notice the payphones where
I called Metallica
Photo Courtesy Fritch Clark

Lips at RnR Heaven
Photo Courtesy The Old Bridge Militia Archives

Anvil - Friday 13, 1982
Photo Courtesy Kevin Hodapp / Frank White Photo Agency

Lips at Friday 13th RockShow
Photo Courtesy The Old
Bridge Militia Archives

Prey opened for Anvil
Photo Courtesy The Old
Bridge Militia Archives

Marsha and Lips getting
deep backstage
Photo Courtesy Kevin Hodapp
/ Frank White Photo Agency

The Mighty Jethro and me
Photo Courtesy The Old
Bridge Militia Archives

Mantas, Cronos, and Rikki
Photo Courtesy Tracey Rayfield

James' first time at RnR Heaven

Backstage at Willy's
Photo Courtesy Metallica photographer Kevin Hodapp

Some of the early shows

Photo Courtesy Gregory Moench
Rock n' Roll Heaven Archives

Photo Courtesy
Gregory Moench
Rock n' Roll
Heaven Archives

Historic poster from the show
Photo Courtesy Gregory Moench RocknRoll Heaven Archives

Venom live at the Paramount
Photo Courtesy Danny Falcon / Frank White Photo Agency

Venom live at the Paramount
Photo Courtesy Kevin Hodapp
/ Frank White Photo Agency

Venom live at the Paramount
Photo Courtesy Kevin Hodapp
/ Frank White Photo Agency

Manowar's Ross the Boss
Photo Courtesy Matthias Prill

Manowar signing in
blood to Megaforce
Photo Courtesy Geoff Thomas

L'amour The Rock Capital of Bklyn
Photo Courtesy Ed Rsposito

Cliff raging at Skateway 9
Photo Courtesy Kevin Hodapp / Frank White Photo Agency

Metallica in Rt 18 Market parking lot
Photo Courtesy Tracey Rayfield

Early Megaforce propaganda

Photo Courtesy Gregory Moench
Rock n' Roll Heaven Archives

Photo Courtesy Gregory
Moench Rock n' Roll
Heaven Archives

TOP 10 SELLERS OF ROCK & ROLL HEAVEN 1985

1. OVERKILL EP
2. S.O.D.•SPEAK ENGLISH OR DIE
3. SLAYER•HELL AWAITS
4. EXODUS•BONDED BY BLOOD
5. C.O.C.•ANIMOSITY
6. SADOM•IN THE SIGN OF EVIL
7. A.O.D.•THE WACKY HI-JINKS
8. OVERKILL•FEEL THE FIRE
9. ANTHRAX•SPREADING THE DISEASE
10. CELTIC FROST• TO MEGAPHERION

Photo Courtesy Gregory
Moench Rock n' Roll
Heaven Archives

Photo Courtesy Gregory
Moench Rock n' Roll
Heaven Archives

Photo Courtesy Gregory
Moench Rock n' Roll
Heaven Archives

Photo Courtesy Gregory
Moench Rock n' Roll
Heaven Archives

Photo Courtesy Gregory
Moench Rock n' Roll
Heaven Archives

Photo Courtesy Gregory
Moench Rock n' Roll
Heaven Archives

My early office
Photo Courtesy Frank White / Frank White Photo Agency

Tony Incigeri and Marsha at work
Photo Courtesy Frank White / Frank White Photo Agency

The only business card we ever had
Photo Courtesy Gregory Moench Rock n' Roll Heaven Archives

The Halloween Headbangers
Ball Concert poster
Photo Courtesy Gregory Moench Rock
n' Roll Heaven ArchivesPhoto Gregg

Riot at the Halloween Head Banger's Ball
Photo Courtesy The Old Bridge Militia Archives

CHICAGO, ILLINOIS - DECEMBER 8, 1983: Raven performing
at The Metro in Chicago, Illinois on December 8, 1983.
Photo Courtesy Gene Ambo

Raven meets Santa
Photo Courtesy Geoff Thomas

First UK show

Metallica making noise in the UK
Photo Courtesy Mike Rijswijk

Metallica live at Roseland
Photo Courtesy Gary Schwartz

Metallica live at Roseland
Photo Courtesy Gary Schwartz

Marsha and Metal Maria
in Amsterdam

Metal Mike and me. Metal Mike has been there
day one with his Dutch magazine Aardshok
Photo Courtesy Mike Rijswijk

Exciter's Dan Beehler
and me in the UK
Photo Courtesy Matthias Prill

Old Bridge Militia '83
Photo Courtesy The Old
Bridge Militia Archives

Neil Turbin and "Bulldozer" Bob In '83
Photo Courtesy Joe Chimiente and the OBMF

Brian Nyers air guitaring to Slayer
Photo Courtesy The Old Bridge Militia Archives

Bobby Blitz and Bulldozer Bob
Photo Courtesy The Old
Bridge Militia Archives

Metal Joe and Lips
Photo Courtesy The Old Bridge Militia Archives

The Fun House where it all happened
Photo Courtesy The Old
Bridge Militia Archives

The notorious 516
Photo Courtesy The Old
Bridge Militia Archives

Ray Dill, Marsha, me, Metal Joe, and Bobby Oujo unite
Photo Courtesy Fritch Clark

The store in Clark, N.J.
Photo Courtesy Brian Nyers

Early Overkill
Photo Courtesy Kevin Hodapp / Frank White Photo Agency

Blitz and me
Photo Courtesy Frank White / Frank White Photo Agency

Blessed Death Larry
doing vocals
Photo Courtesy The Old
Bridge Militia Archives

King Diamond at L'Amours
Photo Courtesy The Old
Bridge Militia Archives

Anthrax on the Europe
Among the Living tour
Photos Courtesy Uwe
'Buffo' Schnadelbach

Anthrax celebrating State of Euphoria going gold
Photo Courtesy Frank White / Frank White Photo Agency

Live at the Megaforce 5th anniversary party
Photo Courtesy Frank White / Frank White Photo Agency

Ace signs to Megaforce
Photo Courtesy Ron Akiyama

Ace and me hanging out
Photo Courtesy Mark Weiss

Hanging with Scott Ian
Photo Courtesy Mark Weiss

Kings X hanging out at the Mega-office
Photo Courtesy Ron Akiyama

Name them all. Anthrax, Slayer, Guns n' Roses,
Metallica, and us
Photo Courtesy Gene Ambo

Overkill's Blitz and DD hanging at the house
Photo Courtesy Frank White / Frank White Photo Agency

Testament Souls of Black
Photo Courtesy Frank White / Frank White Photo Agency

Marsha and me on stage
at "Monsters of Rock" UK
Photo Courtesy Gene Ambo

May 11th. Hurricane Sandy
event presentation cake

"Metal" Maria and me on my 60th birthday
Photo Courtesy John Wicker

Art Ring "Roadie of Death" in 2018

Marsha and me on tour
Photo Courtesy Mark Weiss

Marsha and the Manalapan N.J. Office

Our Mega-crew

Photo Courtesy Ron Akiyama

The Zazula family on
tour together
Photo Courtesy Gene Ambo

The Zazulas arrive in New Hope, PA

The Zazulas on tour
Photo Courtesy Danielle Zazula

Blaire's Playground
Lollapalooza 92
Photo Courtesy Zazula Archives

The Z's promoting Metal Hammer,
a German Metal Magazine
Photo Courtesy Danielle Zazula

Danielle and Frankie Bello
Photo Courtesy Danielle Zazula

Hanging with the Billys
Photo Courtesy Marsha Zazula

Marsha and Tiffany Billy

Soilwork's Björn
Strid and me

Marcos from Shattered Sun
Photo Courtesy Michelle
lee Morales

The Exodus Selfie
Photo Courtesy Gary Schwartz

Venom Inc : Mantas and Demo Man
Tony Dolan raging on stage
Photo Courtesy Fernando Serani
Photography / MetalEyeWitness.com

Chilling with 'Tallica
Photo Courtesy Bob Nalbandian

Talking about some heavy stuff
Photo Courtesy Bob Nalbandian

Inducted into the Hall of Heavy Metal
History at the Marriott Delta in Garden
Grove, CA on January 23rd, 2019

Photo Courtesy Paul Hebert and Ron Lyon

Photo Courtesy Paul Hebert and Ron Lyon

CHAPTER 9

BLAST OFF

IN MARCH OF 1987, MEGAFORCE released their first album through Atlantic Records. It was Overkill's second full length album, "Taking Over." I remember sales weren't through the roof, but there was enough of a buzz around the band to keep Atlantic happily involved and there were enough sales to show the band had potential for growth. Remember this was the early days of Overkill. Everything was a struggle and this was the first time we got to work with Atlantic. We at Megaforce got to work with Atlantic's video department and together we filmed a video for the song "In Union We Stand." It wasn't my pick but Atlantic Records were making promises to me that they would really get behind the song. I, on the other hand, would've went with "Wrecking Crew," but that fell on deaf ears. I must admit the Atlantic machine did help a lot along with the Megaforce offices to get "Taking Over" lots of press and #1 on the metal indie radio charts. We at Megaforce felt that if we could've gotten more albums on the shelves we would've sold more Overkill initially than we did.

While business was going as usual, it came to our attention in late '86 that there were many bands and entities under the name The Legacy. The label went into an agonizing selection process of new names to present to the band. Finally, it was Billy Milano who said we should name the group "Testament" and of course the rest is history. Testament released their first album, ironically called "The Legacy" in April of 1987. I remember being so proud of how the record turned out and right away sent postcards out to my mailing list of thousands saying, "In 1983 came Metallica, and in 1987 comes Testament." We believed in the album very much and had decent sales out of the box. I remember at one point Marsha and I were roaming the halls of Atlantic Records and Jason Flom and David Glew approached me on my marketing of Megaforce bands. They said to me they seemed to sell X amount and no more, just because they're on the label. I responded that if they gave me a little extra money to market the band at retail they would see a growth in sales. This was my argument about Overkill's lack of presence at retail. I argued that the records can't be found therefore they can't be bought. They finally gave me a small budget to market Testament as I requested, a mere five thousand dollars. We were able to spread that five thousand like it was one hundred thousand and ten days later I was called into Atlantic because they wanted to know why Testament sold 47,000 units in such a short period. That was 30,000 more than we originally looked at ten days prior. Due to this realization, Atlantic Records also gave Overkill some retail love and the label was on its way. As the respect between Atlantic and Megaforce grew, so did the roster we were developing. Our Vice-President Ed Trunk came to me to sign Ace Frehley to Megaforce Records and we blasted into outer space together.

THE STORY OF ED TRUNK

I met a young kid at Rock n Roll Heaven by the name of Ed Trunk around 1982. He would frequent the store looking to buy more music than what was available at the music store at the mall and we would recommend him all this great new European music that would blow his mind. Some stuff he liked and other stuff he didn't. Regardless, he was consistent in his desire to find new music and we would supply it for him. When I found out he was DJing a local New Jersey radio station dedicated to heavy metal I started giving him some of my records to play live on the air. This, I thought smartly, would give more exposure to these underground bands that would never find airtime on mainstream stations. So Ed would come to the store to buy records and I would throw in some extra ones for free. This was a very early form of promo he was doing for me.

After Kill 'Em All came out I was having a hard time finding any radio that would be willing to play a single from the album let alone the whole record. We had released the "Jump in the Fire" 12" single and just when I was about to give up I thought of Ed's show. So I drove about an hour and a half in the pouring rain to the radio station on Route 10 in Dover, NJ unannounced with the record under my arm. It turned out the "station" was located inside a very small house, but there I was knocking on the door waiting for the world to listen to this music. Ed, who was in the middle of a show, answered and looked at me with a confused face that said, "What the fuck is the guy from the flea market doing here?" I asked if he could play this record for me and that the band would gain a bigger exposure if he helped me out. He agreed to listen to the record and give it a shot next week but I was persistent that

125

I wanted the record to be played at that very moment. I believed in Metallica and knew with limited radio we were going to have to fight daily to get as much exposure as we could. Once the single was played, I took the record and signed it for Ed:

"Ed, you were the first. Thank you—Jon Z"

I told Ed that if this Megaforce thing ever picked up and we had enough money to hire people I would hire him. He must've thought I was messing around or just being kind but sometime in late 1984 I was true to my promise. When I offered Ed a job I let him know the good and bad news. The good news was that after a deal we made with Metallica we had enough money to hire him, but the bad news was he wasn't going to be working with Metallica. Poor Ed thought we were fully staffed in some nice big office only to realize we were still working out of our home in Old Bridge. He went from working inside one house to working at another. I put Ed to work with the rest of us and had him work with his radio connections. He would call stations and try to have Megaforce artist played and it was again our early form of promotion through the airwaves. Ed would also get in contact with retailers and chain stores to have our records available for sale through them. Again, we didn't know what the hell we were doing but we worked endlessly for these bands and tried everything to persuade the major retail chains to come play with us which they eventually did.

Very soon as luck would have it I was having a lot of success managing our bands and wanted to take a step away from the daily grind at Megaforce. I promoted Ed to Vice-President and gave him a company card to buy a suit at Macy's. I figured since he was going to be taking business meetings with Atlantic Records and represent us as a liaison he should do so in a presentable way for our company. We were all casual guys in jeans and t-shirts but I wasn't about to let Ed talk to Atlantic's president dressed that way. I got a kick out of sending Ed in a suit to represent us to Atlantic! It was very funny to me because I hated suits so much.

One day while working in our new office in East Brunswick, NJ, Ed started talking to me about branching out our talent. He suggested going after some crossover mainstream acts that would get airtime exposure but still be respected by our world of underground fans. It would be an understatement to say Ed was a KISS fan. He adored and worshipped them. So when their lead guitarist, Ace Frehley, parted ways with KISS, Ed asked me about potentially bringing him in. Ace was considered a huge liability because there were so many rumors about him being unworkable, out of his mind, an alcoholic and major drug user—basically that it would be a nightmare to work with him. Eddie Kramer was spending time with Ace and vouched he was in shape but Ed and I wanted to make sure he had all his marbles, so we all had a lunch meeting down at the Rockefeller skating rink where there was a restaurant downstairs. As soon as we walked into the place, everyone there recognized him, calling out his birth name, Paul. It was a very warm and welcoming mood. As we ordered our meals, Ace asked the waiter if he could get two pieces of bread with tuna fish in the middle. The waiter looked at him a bit confused and asked, "Sir, do you mean a tuna fish sandwich?" Looking back, I still laugh at that moment. We spoke and things seemed to run over smoothly. Ace was looking for a label that would believe in him and there was no doubt in our minds he could still play and sell out venues. He was also in great condition. On our drive back home Ed and I discussed the positives and negatives and ultimately the decision was mine to make.

Ace Frehley would become another member of our MegaFamily.

After Frehley's Comet hit earth, the album did very well both in sales and through fans alike. We found out one day the album was sitting somewhere near 475,000 units so we were just inches away from a Gold record for half a million sales. At such a close number of sales needed we decided to start a marketing campaign dubbed "The Race For Ace." We made t-shirts, called up retailers, promoted on all medias, stickers, you name it and it most likely had a "Race For Ace" logo on it. Unfortunately, retailers were sitting on more copies than they could sell, so in those days you could return them and get your money back. What ended up happening was the sales starting going backwards from 475,000. So the "Race For Ace" became more about maintaining him to where he was. It was about 30 years ago and I bet those sales would surely be over half a million by this point.

By the second album Ace had fallen off the wagon. This was not the way it was on the first album and it showed in his performance. The backing band wrote most of the material because Ace just couldn't show up during those sessions. Added to that we had secured a spot for Ace on Iron Maiden's upcoming tour, so the second album was really pushed through the doors. This whole album was rushed so quickly that according to Ed we ended up just purchasing a stock photo from NASA for the album cover because we had no time to hire an artist. Once the record was released it was a massive commercial failure and we were not too surprised considering the recording process of it A third and final album *Trouble Walkin'* was released the following year. Even with Eddie Kramer back at the helm this time and guitarist Richie Scarlet in the band, unfortunately we couldn't get back the momentum we got on the first album and we parted company with Ace soon after

As Frehley's Comet was in full orbit, Megaforce and Overkill decided to do something very much unprecedented at the time. The Parents Music Resources Center, PMRC, was really busting everybody's bubbles over lyrical content dubbed obscene to children's ears. We didn't care and released the S.O.D album under the radar but now knowing Atlantic Records' lyrical stand on explicit lyrics, we went to them to let them know Megaforce planned to release an E.P by Overkill entitled "!!!FUCK YOU!!!" Atlantic asked us immediately not do this and to take the E.P somewhere else. In the fall of '87, Megaforce Records, through our independent distributor Caroline, released the "!!!FUCK YOU!!!" E.P. in all its splendor. I have no recollection of anybody complaining or even making a fuss about it. In some markets we did have to cover the album artwork with a black plastic bag and a sticker but when you opened the bag you got the middle finger. The record sold well based on its own merit and the band continued to grow in popularity.

Around the time of the !!!FUCK YOU!!! E.P., Megaforce and Caroline got ready for another act that was sure to make a statement in the musical community. Billy Milano put together his own band, Method Of Destruction, and released their first full length album, "U.S.A for M.O.D." The band featured John Monte on bass, Louis Svitek on guitar and drummer Tim Mallare. They backed Billy on both the studio and touring all the way until their third release. That first album was well received and Billy Milano was able to retain his notoriety achieved during the S.O.D days. They toured the U.S.A album and grew in popularity which set everyone up for the release of my favorite Megaforce record ever, "Surfin' M.O.D." I remember how much I enjoyed the brilliance that went into the making of that record. From "Goldfish from Hell" to "Color My World," this E.P *rocks.*

Meanwhile on the Anthrax front, the band was busy breaking in Europe. One of the highlights of my life was when Anthrax played Donnington Speedway in the U.K to 92,000 people opening for Bon Jovi and Metallica. I remembered it rained and the mud was intense but it was clear to see from these show where both Metallica and Anthrax were headed. It seemed like their rise was evident. In fact, "Ride the Lightning" was certified Gold by November of that year which added even more validity to the metal movement I was representing.

Blaire, our youngest daughter was born in July of this year. She was the cutest ginger you'd ever want to see and soon Marsha and our new daughter continued with the flow of 1987 .We were now a family of five and this was a blessed time. Things were getting brighter with my growing family; me and all my girls.

I felt like there was no stopping me. With Marsha by my side and the organization of friends and young minds that were Megaforce, I was starting to feel invincible. This may all seem wonderful to the public but I am a manic depressive and I was riding a rocket ship of mania which for me at that time had no end in sight.

CHAPTER 10

MEGAFORCE GOES TO NEBRASKA

ONE EVENING AROUND MY BIRTHDAY I had one of my 3:30 a.m. awakenings from sleep. I remember so clearly a voice saying to me, "Jonnny, you have to throw a MAJOR party." Not a birthday party for me but a 5th year anniversary party for the label. As soon as it was possible I got up and called all the Mega-bands to see if they would want to play at this party. Once again I was doing this without figuring costs and logistics. I had to pay to have every band fly in from all over the country to play. I produced it like a festival and I believe I only charged $20 for tickets for the floor and I had the balcony of the Ritz reserved for the VIP and press people who I flew in from all over the world. I was a real show-off and I put everybody up at the Mayflower Hotel in New York City. I can't imagine how many rooms we rented for 2-3 nights for some of our guests. The party was to celebrate how far we had come in 5 years and I think it costed more than $40,000 for the event before it was over. We didn't make any money from it, that's for sure. Even though the show sold out the expenses were way too much. We even had street vendors come inside to give out hot dogs, chips and soda up in the balcony section. The whole party was an ego trip for me. I wanted to show how far we came in 5 years as I was riding a wave of mania and success. I felt GOD was on my side. Every voice that spoke to me inside my head, I followed, and it all turned out like the right move. Plus, I was doing a lot of drugs. This depicts the time and place of where I was at mentally.

While Testament were playing they had problems with their amps and in anger knocked them down all over the stage. This caused a big problem because the party was like a festival and everybody was to share the backline. I remember the music playing and then stopping. I ran to see what was going on and was told "fuck you" by a band member. I just figured that you can't do good even when you try. I felt like, "what the fuck?" You can't make everybody happy...EVER! Thank GOD we managed to get things back in working order and the show finished without a hitch, just with massive stress.

There was some jealousy among the ranks in the bands within the Megaforce family. Not many bands had nice things to say about the other bands which was a weird thing to me because I loved them all. I was hurt when bands would say nasty things about others. Bands would get upset if I ever said something nice about another band, always giving me "The Look." Marsha has a degree in child psychology so she was great at assisting others through her patience. Her ability to communicate prohibited many problems throughout that time. People spoke differently to Marsha than they did to me and that is what kept things going. Marsha was like a mother confessor, while I was insane during those times. I didn't go as deep as Marsha. When I did I always seemed to say the wrong things. She doused fires between me and bands, me and partners, me and the world. I felt like I was a bull in a china shop knocking everything around and Marsha was right there making sure nothing broke or got knocked off the shelf.

The night after the party we had a listening party for the new upcoming Anthrax album, *State of Euphoria*. I had all the press come down to another club in New York to listen to it.

The band was getting bigger at that time and their albums were now starting to go Gold. There was much attention to the new album by the press and there was particular interest to the song

"Anti-Social" which was written by the French band Trust.

I flew to Paris to meet with Bernie Bonvoisin and Nono Krief from Trust and we discussed the possibility of doing a single together with Anthrax. He said he would be very thrilled and honored for that to happen. I remember as a result that song went on the album. While touring the world with Iron Maiden in France, Trust also played on the bill and they performed "Anti-Social" together. That was a great night.

In 1989 we made a deal with MTV's Headbangers Ball Show to tour America. It included Anthrax, Exodus and Helloween. This was a very successful tour and established Anthrax as a headliner in midsize theaters in the U.S. During that time the band toured the shit out of the world. It was fantastic. This period brought a Metal Renaissance to the music business because everybody was finally smelling the money and the bands were making great music. One couldn't deny the other. The scene grew into an industry and we were part of the major label system through Atlantic and Island Records. Metal was growing organically, the proper way. Only some of the hair bands from L.A., who seemed more manufactured at the time, were gaining the MTV and radio spotlights that were still not available to Anthrax, Slayer and other bands of

133

that genre. They were true to the revolution and the bands we had on Megaforce demonstrated you could still succeed by going 10 yards at a time without the need for radio or MTV regular rotation.

THE LIFE AND TIMES OF VIO·LENCE

It's funny that when asked to tell the story of Vio-lence on Megaforce Records I go blank. However, this is what I do remember: There was an important figure in the Vio-lence hierarchy named Debbie Abono, a woman dedicated to the metal cause and soft spoken. Even though Debbie was this sweet, kind and wonderful woman, she was always powerful enough in getting her point across. It was Debbie who introduced me to Vio-lence, who at the time were having a hard time on the MCA Mechanix label. She brought them to me to grab the ball and run with it once they were free from their prior label. I was always intrigued by Vio-lence and working with Debbie was something I wanted to do, so off to The Bay Area we went again. Marsha and I landed at the Oakland Airport and quickly headed to Union City to see the band. I found them in a storage facility. They were rehearsing when we got there and right away I could tell these were great musicians. Their guitarists Robb Flynn and Phil Demmel, who later played together again in Machine Head, were a great guitar duo. I was very keen on signing them to the label, and then, it happened. I loved the music but I was having a terrible time with the vocals. I just couldn't wrap my head around them but I felt that it could just be me and accepted the band, lock stock and singer. Never did I expect what was soon to come. Atlantic Records had a major problem with the album cover and wouldn't distribute the album called "Oppressing the Masses" because of its violent artwork. We already printed several thousand covers and were ready to ship when Atlantic came to me freaking out on the lyrics to a song, Torture Tactics, which featured some pretty detailed violence that Atlantic Records thought was brutal and had crossed the line. We were told we should scrap the entire project. Instead of scrapping it we changed the cover art and removed the song Torture Tactics from all remaining prints. Unfortunately, once their album came out it didn't do very well in sales. Atlantic felt this was a break in Megaforce's lucky streak and brought a weird vibe to the Megaforce/Atlantic relationship. During all this, the band's manager Debbie Abono was ill and there was great confusion and indecision. My head was always on the chopping block. You barely had a handshake if you were doing well and when it was bad we were always certainly told about it under no uncertain terms.

The blind trust between Atlantic and Megaforce began to fade and I couldn't blame Atlantic for wanting the best from us. I may have been a little caught up in my own hype and I was feeling invincible and my creative juices continued to overflow. Megaforce still went forward and put the song "Torture Tactics" out through its indie arm Caroline as a 12". Even though this was a bold move it was so bleak that the band's second release, "Nothing To Gain," was never released by us. I was discouraged yet we plodded ahead, always seeking what we thought were the greatest unsigned bands in our lifetime.

Just to make the matters completely insane with Atlantic Records and Megaforce, I decided to open a classical music label in our Megaforce family. That's right, I said it, *classical music*. My brother Evan lived in NYC and one day while visiting his apartment I heard this amazing piano playing in the hallway. I was blown away and asked my brother who's making all that ruckus. He told me it was a pianist named John Bayless who was a master of the classics and a recording artist. John had several albums out on the Pro Arte label. He had recorded Beatles classics, each song performed in the style of one of the great composers. It was brilliant. I really wanted to meet this man so Evan arranged it for Marsha and I to visit him in his apartment.

It was quite an experience at first. John had a small studio with a giant Grand Piano right in the middle of the room. It was way too big. A 5-foot baby grand piano would have sufficed but this was a 9 foot Baldwin. It took up his whole place. So we hung around and it turned out his deal with Pro Arte was coming to an end. I found out he was a protege of the great Composer Conductor of the New York Philharmonic, Leonard Bernstein, and was to be a guest pianist for Bernstein's performance of Requiem at Carnegie Hall. This stuff blew my mind and then a voice came in my head that asked me, out of the blue, to ask John what he thought of Bruce Springsteen. Next thing we were joking about doing a Springsteen Concerto. Bayless could take the Springsteen classics and do them in the styles of the great composers. We went into a creative mania. Our minds were peaking with ideas. We gave this project our best and recorded an album. If you're lucky you might even find one. I don't think it ever came out on CD. One of our biggest obstacles was that in retail there was no section to put this album on display. The classical buyers hated it and the pop buyers didn't know what to make of it and the radio stations who played classical music wouldn't play it. We still sold close to 8,000 copies but it was a bitch. I remember the famed Chairman, Ahmet Ertegun of Atlantic Records, calling me into his office. He asked what I was doing and advised me to focus on what music I know best.

Ahmet also told me he thought I was wasting time and money. Of course I didn't listen to him. The great Leonard Bernstein had passed away and I wanted to produce a Leonard Bernstein tribute album and I did. My new label under Atlantic/Megaforce was named Megaforte Records. I was out of my mind and I was really tripping on this.

We had a great agent at ICM, Ed Micone, and Bayless opened for Alan King and Howie Mandel which exposed me to doing shows in Atlantic City and the Westbury Music Fair. It was very different and it was quite an enchanting experience. Unfortunately, my real world got super busy and my charmed life with John Bayless came to a long sabbatical. The Bernstein tribute was never released on Megaforte. "Greetings from John Bayless" was released in Oct of 1988. Atlantic was never happy Megaforce made such a sidestep and this was not the first time that there were disagreements between Atlantic and Megaforce.

THE KING IS COMING

Marsha received a tape in the mail from an S.Taylor and we thought it was the Steve Taylor who was a keyboard player we admired in a band called DeGarmo and Key. I played it after Marsha did and I didn't think much of it. I felt it was missing something. Marsha kept it from me but played it when she was in her car. Something in the music grabbed her ears big time. She kept it to herself until she realized this was too good not to be on Megaforce. The person who had sent the tape was not who she thought it was and after some phone calls got in touch with their then manager Sam Taylor (S. Taylor) who was looking for a label for his band, King's X. He sent us a video and that's when she hit me with the band. I really admired and loved bands that did things for themselves like shoot their own videos and produce their own music. I gave in and let her plead her case and once I saw the video I understood her excitement. So we went down to Houston, TX to see King's X play and they were fantastic and we fell in love. We knew it would be a hard road with the band because of how different the music was. They were real pioneers to drop D tuning, the grunge movement, and incorporated harmonies from all three musicians in their progressive style of music. Doug Morris, the president and CEO of Atlantic, would ask me about King's X. Every musician on Atlantic wanted to know everything about this band because every band loved them. He was astonished by how highly musicians thought of them. Everybody knew it was special but no one knew how to break it, including me. We made great videos for the band through Sam Taylor which MTV loved. They even went on tour with AC/DC to no avail. Still in all we managed to sell greater numbers as time went on. It was a slow grow. The one thing that grew all the time, however, was their street credibility and respect. That is why they still successfully tour the United States today.

I felt that the voice in my head kept telling me to move forward. I felt that sometimes the world wasn't ready for my musical ears. I had been right so far and I kept on picking winners but the world wasn't ready for *all* my choices. This was very hard to accept. I worked King's X like a dog and it took a while. We sold a good amount of records but it still didn't break through the way we had hoped or expected. Yet to many this band is of legendary status.

As '89 closed we were in high anticipation for the new M.O.D. record on Megaforce/Caroline. It was the band's second full length offering and once again there were some very controversial topics on the album. I never censored my artists and I never would, it wasn't my place to do so. What was really great about these M.O.D. albums lyrically is the delivery was beyond brilliant, even if you didn't agree with what Billy was saying.

In songs like "Don't Feed the Bears" you could feel the humor while the song had a dark, dark edge. We did a photo shoot with the band at the Great Bear Water Company in New Jersey. I don't remember but I think the photo shoot was so brutal that pedestrians thought it was real and called the police on us. The shoot had a bear mauling the band with blood all over the place. People thought it was a mob hit.

CHAPTER 11

TURN IT UP

I N 1990 WE CONTINUED TO work on projects from '89 and before. One of the most important things for me was to set up Anthrax's new album *Persistence of Time* due out in August of that year. Much time was spent traveling to every country in Europe, setting up the promotion for their forthcoming release. This time we expected big numbers from day one. It was my goal to break the Top 10 Billboard Chart and debut on all the other charts around the world. A lot of time was spent plotting out their European campaigns and no detail was left to anyone's imagination. There were, I believe, five different configurations for the "In My World" single alone. It was an amazing campaign.

When I returned to the states my agent Jeff Rowland contacted me and discussed a traveling festival. It would feature three of the top 4 Metal bands on the scene who would rotate the second, third and fourth position every night and there would be a strong band opening the show. The bands would tour under the name "Clash of the Titans" and the bill would be all headlining with equal logos and cooperation. Slayer, Megadeth and Anthrax would headline and Alice in

Chains were selected by all three managers to open the show. It was very interesting for me to work alongside Rick Sales who managed Slayer and Ron Lafitte who managed Megadeth and see how they operated. There were no ego clashes, just three guys representing their bands and we were all fair to each other. It was a true pleasure working alongside these gentlemen. History will say this was a very successful tour and it certainly opened the doors for the "Big 4" concerts that happened later on. I thought this would be the biggest endeavor in my career, but just two years later we were an integral part of Lollapalooza 2 with Ministry, a band we managed at the time and who were even more of a spectacle.

Persistence of Time peaked at #24 on the Billboard Charts and went Gold. Anthrax were established as a band to be reckoned with, yet I was still having trouble establishing them as their own headliner in an arena capacity. This was frustrating for me and I'm sure the band relented over the situation as well.

Souls of Black reared its head by metal/thrash masters Testament in October of that same year. It came out in a rush due to the fact that they were to go on tour with Judas Priest if they could get a record out quickly. It all turned out good in the end.

This was soon followed by King's X's *Faith. Hope. Love.* Once again King's X delivered a great album followed by fantastic videos and touring. Megaforce did get them some radio and MTV play, but we still couldn't break the band. For those of you who are reading this and haven't heard a Kings X recording, it's time to give their music a serious listen. You may be awed.

In February of 1991 both Anthrax and Suicidal Tendencies were nominated for the prestigious Grammy awards. Anthrax for *Persistence of Time* and Suicidal for *Lights...Camera...Revolution!* Believe it or not Marsha and I managed S.T. for about nine months. I don't even know how we became their managers but I think David Glew, who was running Epic Records at the time, called me and told me I should manage them, and it went down pretty easily. We were fans of the band and spoke to vocalist Mike Muir on the phone. Next thing you know we found ourselves down in L.A. doing a photo shoot with them for their forthcoming album. I remember it was a great shoot down in the freight yards. The title of the album, I think, was something I came up with because of a photo shoot that was held on top of the marque of some old run-down movie theater. Lights... Cameras...Revolution. We even went to the Grammy's together. What a hoot, but problems soon came to light when one person in the band, who I've known over the years, came to me for a favor that I said yes to, but I had also turned someone else in the band down on. The misunderstanding lead to confusion which made it uncomfortable to continue in our relationship. Mike, bassist Rob Trujillo and guitarist Rocky George and I still remain friends today although I must admit Rocky has always been a special friend to me. It's also kind of cool that Rob has moved on to play bass with Metallica. He remains one of my favorite bass players. By the way, just to show you how much fun it was managing Suicidal Tendencies: I went to David Glew at Epic and told him Psycho Miko wanted him to put out an altogether different album by an altogether different band called Infectious Grooves. Can you imagine Epic Records entrusted me to keep their band from doing anything crazy, and the first thing I do as manager is tell him about Infectious Grooves? Infectious Grooves were an amazing band and they would've been fun to manage if we stayed on. The nine months sort of went like that, wild times at the Grammys, photo shoots, touring, drama, side bands, an amazing album, all in and out before we had time to blink.

MINDFUNK AND THE SPACE CAKE

After bassist John Monte and guitarist Louis Svitek were no longer in M.O.D. they contacted me about wanting to release new music under a project they had been working on with Reed St. Mark, former drummer of Celtic Frost. I took a photographer to the basement of my house to shoot John and Louis jamming to get promotional photos for the press. We had a great shot of both John and Louis sitting next to each other with a light bulb burning over their heads. John, who was a smoker, had filled up the room with a cloud of deep thought that made for an impressive shot. We sent them all over the world for the press to see. The press were shocked when we delivered the name of the new project we were cooking at Casa Z, "MindFuck." We realized the name was a little abrasive so we changed it to MindFunk, although the band was indeed a total mindfuck. As we were looking for a vocalist, our friend Mike Gitter recommended Pat Dubar from California punk band Uniform Choice. It took a while for Pat to get into the groove of things but once he got it we were good to move forward. MindFunk would rehearse in Hackensack, NJ, in an industrial area and I would send every A&R person from every label to check out the band. It felt like we had new people showing up every day, and every one of them wanted to sign the band. It became so crazy that Richard Branson called my house to tell me how great this band would be on Virgin Records. We ultimately decided to take the band to Epic. The contract we negotiated was so good we heard it was brought up in an Epic lawyers meeting as an example of a contract to never agree to again !

We had some success with our first album which sold about 127,000 units, which is great at an independent records level but for Epic Records, wasn't Michael Jackson numbers. Epic also assigned Pearl Jam's A&R guy to MindFunk and he tried to make them more like Pearl Jam. As a result of this, and low album sales, MindFunk were dropped from Epic. Producer Terry Date was coming hot off his Pantera releases and we were fortunate to work with him on the second album in Seattle which Megaforce ended up releasing. Their second album didn't do so well either and by the time we got to the third album there was a whole different MindFunk that existed. Jason Cappola and Reed were replaced and it wasn't the same band. The management and band were losing interest in each other. Eventually the band broke up. Right before the end, in a desperate attempt to save the band, both MindFunk and Nudeswirl toured Europe together. Nudeswirl would beat each other up onstage, while MindFunk was starting to get discouraged. By the time I went to check on the bands in Paris it was turning into the tour of hate.

To mellow ourselves out from the European tour, Art Ring and Marsha went out to purchase some pot brownies while in Amsterdam at Picasso's bakery. While they were interviewing, we decided to eat big pieces of cake to crave our hunger. Two hours later when we met up with the band we were tripping terribly because we found out much later it wasn't pot cake but acid cake. The band didn't know this and they started eating the cake as well and started tripping as hard as us. To make matters worse we all got invited by Epic to join them for dinner which we couldn't refuse. Before we left for dinner we started smoking hash which really twisted our minds. As we were going down the elevator we all thought, "how the hell are supposed to go have dinner with Epic?" We were all tripping our brains out and we couldn't let Epic's people see us this stoned. We had sent out two scouts to check the first floor to make sure we could sneak out of the hotel quick enough to not cause a scene. We heard the coast was clear so we ran to the elevator only to see Epic staff waiting by the elevator as well. We bolted back to the room and waited until they were gone and then snuck out the side door. Once we made it to dinner we noticed we were all underdressed in our shorts and black t-shirts so I borrowed Pat Dubar's sports jacket which was quite tight on me. He was a size 46 and I'm a 56 and I was walking around the place looking like Frankenstein's monster. I was too stoned and cold to take this ridiculous jacket off. My mouth started to get very dry so I went with Monte to get water from a Dutch Gift shop where a man who spoke no English gave me water out of pity. All I could say was, "Wwaaah waah, waaah wahhh," because of my mouth being so parched. Once that was over we walked across the street to an Indian restaurant where they had these little tables, like a setup for dolls and toys. Monte says to me in a very serious tone, "No Jon, I don't believe we'll be sitting here." I laughed my ass off with the rest of the guys who the acid cake hadn't fully hit yet. They were still riding on the hash they'd smoked. We found a huge table for all of us to sit at. There we all were with Marsha, Art, Maria and MindFunk when the acid cake hits the entire table like a tidal wave at the same time. They all start acting like army soldiers with long southern drawls. It was really freaking me out and giving me the shakes. It was too much for me to handle so I gave Maria my credit card and told her to take care of the guys and asked Marsha to get me the fuck to my bed because I was done for the night. I found out later that MindFunk didn't even eat at the restaurant and left after I did to trip around Amsterdam leaving Maria behind with all the food they ordered. Marsha and I were lost in the Red-Light District looking for our hotel when finally, I asked her to get us a cab because I thought through my paranoia that people were out to kill me, coming out of the alleys or from the little holes in the buildings. We ended up taking a cab for just one-half a city block. Once we were settled in our room we called the MindFunk hotel room to check in on them only to find out they were under the covers of the bed in their room freaking out as well. Art Ring got on the phone and said, "Jonny, that was no pot cake."

MindFunk was poised in my mind to be one of the great bands and it was all kind of weird to watch everything go south. It was a real rollercoaster ride and it made me think if I even had it in me anymore to make the right decisions with Megaforce.

BRING THE NOISE

For as long as I can remember Scott Ian wore a Public Enemy T-Shirt. I questioned him often about being such a huge fan of Rap music. He would usually answer me by having me listen to it. I never connected like he did until he played me *It Takes a Nation of Millions To Hold Us Back* by Public Enemy. The album seemed flawless and believe it or not I found it heavy. I especially got hooked on their DJ, Terminator X. He did some amazing stuff. They all did and then there it was ... just waiting for me to hear it ... "A IS FOR ANTHRAX." That monolithic opus of a song, "Bring the Noise" hit me real hard and then the whole album made sense. I played *It Takes a Nation of Millions* everywhere we went. I don't think I made Marsha too happy, but that album and Faith No More's *Angel Dust* fought for the most played

146

album while driving around our summer home on Long Beach Island, New Jersey.

Things were picking up. Metallica were huge, Megaforce was doing very well and Anthrax were having success as well. It was the beginning of the good times. I don't remember whose idea it was for Anthrax and Public Enemy to join forces and record "Bring the Noise" together. I don't know if it matters but Anthrax were cool enough from their release of "I'm The Man" that it reached the ears of the people I needed to contact to make the collaboration a reality. It may have been Rick Rubin who I went to first but ended up speaking to Russell Simmons. From there I discussed the idea with Don Einer over at Sony, and before I knew it "Bring the Noise" featuring both Anthrax and Public Enemy was to be a reality. I spent a lot of time with them during the recording of the song and was there for the music video. We were interested in a group called The Company who did the video for "Head Like a Hole" by Nine Inch Nails. We went to them and decided to shoot it in Chicago under the "L" where three elevated train lines intersected. You had trains going over the band and sparking over their heads. There was a stage made for Anthrax and Public Enemy to perform in the park that was located directly below the Elevated Trains. Children from the nearby schools came to the shoot plus the people from the neighborhood filled in as the live audience. There was some studio work done with special effects as well and when we put it all together, MTV loved it. It did so well on MTV that it made the "Bring the Noise" tour a reality. It started when the guys told me it would be amazing to tour with Public Enemy and I would try my best to make it come true. We had a dressing room where we changed our clothes and Flavor Flav stored all his clocks and stage wear. Both Chuck D and I were just sitting around waiting for Flav to be ready. While we were sitting there, Chuck and I agreed on how cool this project was and started discussing the possibility of taking it on tour. We decided to have Les Claypool's band Primus open the shows. They were a very cool band and we had to decide on something that would work for both audiences. Primus were doing well on MTV so we put them on. We set the tour price at one thing and I remember getting a phone call from my agent that we have to deal with the prices here because the P.E. camp wanted more money than Anthrax ever charged to perform. It was a real eye opener for me because the promoters decided to pay that money without too big of a fight. Island/Megaforce wanted to make sure there was enough advertisement and marketing so we teamed up with SONY and had an extensive MTV campaign hitting each market individually and nationally.

To test the waters, the very first show of the tour was at the Mid-Hudson Civic Center in Poughkeepsie, NY. We traveled with a crew of maybe six or seven but Public Enemy walked in with about 25-30 guys, and when I asked them what they all did in the group they said they were all part of P.E. I thought to myself how this entire thing would work. We didn't have catering for this many people. But it then came time for P.E. to go onstage and these extra guys really didn't do anything but hang out and do a number with them at the end while the Anthrax crew worked all the production. I remember talking to Chuck about how weird this would be if it continued like this. None of these guys did sound, lights, nothing technical. Chuck was used to all the production being provided in those days and was told this would be provided by the tour. The next step was for me to ask Chuck who amongst his army was most technically inclined. I asked our tour manager and lighting designer, the wonderful Rick Downey, to please have a seat with this gentleman and see what can be done to help P.E. become self-sustained touring machine without the need of our crew.

The lineup was to be Primus, Public Enemy and Anthrax, then P.E. coming back out to play "Bring the Noise" together at the end of Anthrax's set. The shows went down great. There were a lot of white people with P.E. and NWA shirts in the crowd, but not a lot of Anthrax and Metallica shirts on P.E.'s audience. The show was good, but when Anthrax and P.E. came out together it was madness. In L.A., Ice T came out on stage for the finale with everyone at a sold out show at the Irvine Meadows. It went down incredibly. One of the things in my life that I remember most about this P.E./Anthrax combination was that for some reason I had to speak to Chuck D years later and jokingly in the conversation I asked him if he still tours with all those guys. He laughed and told me that they're his production people now and the guy Rick trained is the best light man in the hip hop scene. I wish I knew the guy's name. I'm so happy for him.

Four days prior to the end of the tour we were to perform in Oakland. On October 19th, there was an enormous firestorm that started in Oakland where the concert was taking place the next night. This was a major fire that consumed most of the city and it looked Apocalyptic. We didn't know if we were going to do the show that night but the bands showed up and set up. The promoter, Bill Graham, told us the show must go on, so we proceeded with our plans. It was at this show where I finally got to meet Bill who inspired me and was my hero. He stormed into my room about the attendance not being so great. I said to him this tour has had great attendances and that he should consider the fact there are fires everywhere you look and people might not want to drive through blazes to get here. We talked and continued to argue, then we spoke about people we mutually knew and music we both knew and loved. We walked outside the arena and there were fires everywhere in the distance engulfing the city. Bill told me World War 3 wouldn't stop people from going to a show if they wanted to go, still discussing the attendance. There was nothing left for me to say. I told him what I thought about him as being a legend to me and he smiled. Bill had orchestrated those early Grateful Dead shows including Janis Joplin and Jefferson Airplane. He ran the Fillmore and Fillmore East where I had gotten my early taste of live rock and promoted the American leg of Live Aid in 1985. Needless to say he was an inspiration to me and it was amazing spending time with him. Just five days later, Bill was setting up a benefit concert for the people of Oakland when he died in a helicopter accident. It was kind of weird that I got to meet him at the end of his life. He was *The Man* and it makes me sad every time I think of the nice conversation I had with him while Oakland burned in the background.

CHAPTER 12

GRUNGE KILLS

NIRVANA KNOCKED MICHAEL JACKSON'S "DANGEROUS" from its number 1 spot on the prestigious Billboard charts on January 11, 1992. This was an omen. Soon the entire world would be taken over by the Grunge sound generated out of Seattle, Washington. It was there that a small independent label, Sub-Pop, who were releasing underground alternative music, emerged as giants on the major labels. Bands like Nirvana, Pearl Jam, Alice in Chains and Soundgarden were taking over the music scene and as a result the sales of our once bullet-proof catalogue had diminished considerably. These low sales weren't paying the bills of my staff or the other items that appear on the negative side of any companies' balance sheet. It became apparent Megaforce was in trouble. In 1992 all my costs ran over a million dollars and I had not had a break out act on Megaforce in a while. The label was selling a good amount of product but not enough to be self-sustaining.

In order to keep the label afloat, Marsha and I supported the company's financial needs with the money we earned from our management company and we decided to reach out to another major label who would give us a better deal than the Atlantic renewal offer. I was also starting to hear different sounds in my head other than Metal. After discovering the likes of Testament, Metallica, Raven, Overkill and Anthrax, it was getting harder to find something Metal that was different and challenging to me. Once I was hooked on Kings X my whole attitude towards music changed and I was hoping I could find a new home for Megaforce that would share in our new vision. Although Megaforce was feeling a bit of a financial pinch, Anthrax were rocking the world and were selling a lot of records and our relationships with other companies were at a point where they would throw heaps of money at our bands. Next, we started talking to other companies for the new home of Megaforce.

The deal with Atlantic was coming to an end. Testament, around this time, was about to release *The Ritual* and it remained on Atlantic along with Kings X and Overkill. Only Anthrax remained with Island/ Megaforce and we would start our new world with Polygram as our parent label. The A&R department at Megaforce was better than ever in finding the unique sounds of the time, but not one band was Metal. The Seattle sound was ruling the world and Megaforce's Metal record sales continued to diminish because of it. I felt that Metal was heading back into the dark ages, so instead of continuing to release artists on Megaforce that I didn't care for, we released albums from bands who created music everyone in our office agreed on. The bands at that time were Tribe After Tribe, who played alternative music out of South Africa, Nudeswirl, who played grunge, an industrial metal band named Skatenigs, a funk metal band named Sweaty Nipples out of Portland, and the legendary Warren Haynes from the Allman Brothers and later Government Mule. We put out great albums by these bands but they were costly not only financially but to my mental health.

NUDESWIRL

What a great, talented group of musicians Nudeswirl were. They were discovered in our own backyard, right in New Brunswick, NJ. Yet the recording of their Megaforce debut album was a horror show. We hired a great producer to work with them in the studio and the budget was about $60,000. We were called in to hear the mixes and I flipped out. At first I thought I was losing my mind because it didn't sound right to me. Then everyone started arguing and telling me it was indeed just me who thought it sounded terrible. I had started to doubt my own ears so I had the record mixed over and over until I spent $96,000 on an album I hated. It sounded too good. To me it was some other band's record and I went into a rage and collected all $96,000 worth of tape and work and tossed it into a dumpster never to be seen or heard of again. Short of one hundred thousand dollars spent on a piece of crap went unheard and straight into the trash it went. The screws weren't even loose anymore in my head... they had fallen right out.

The next day I called my friend Eric Rachel at Trax East in South River NJ and asked him if he can deliver me a Nudeswirl album for $15,000. I asked him for an album that actually sounded like them! He did a marvelous job and it was perfection. The record's lead single and video were picked up by MTV and played on Beavis and Butthead regularly. They toured the world with MindFunk but in the end only sold 36,000 records. As an Indie we sold good numbers but as a major label we were really not doing the numbers needed to cover our costs. In the meantime, Megaforce was biting it on the sales from Caroline who were suffering as well from the grunge plague that looked like it wasn't leaving. I highly recommend listening to this Nudeswirl album. It rocks very hard. Marsha and I listened to it the other night and it remains a lot of fun.

Our great hope was Warren Haynes. I originally heard about Warren from my cousin from Nashville, Rhonda. She told me about Warren's work with country outlaw David Allen Coe and his writing with Garth Brooks. Of course his sitting in for Duane Allman alongside Dickie Betts in the Allman Brothers wasn't too shabby, either. Warren came by our office to hang and discuss business when he pulled out a guitar and began playing some of the songs he was going to record on this album. We discussed Chuck Levelle, Eric Clapton's keyboardist, to produce. Then there was a list of The Who's Who of Rock on it. The whole project was very exciting and expensive but Marsha and I went for it, hook line and sinker. The product was worked very hard once it came out by both Polygram and Megaforce but we were too early in Warren's career at both press and the radio. They weren't coming as fast as we needed. The fantastic recording *Tales of Ordinary Madness* soon lost the interest at Polygram and things weren't looking great. It was becoming apparent by the end of 1993 things between Polygram and Megaforce were not healthy. I kept missing the bullseye too many times in a row for it not to become a coincidence. I was losing my touch and everyone knew it.

ELEKTRA

After delivering the required records to Island it was time for Anthrax to shop a new deal. It started to get really out of control once I began shopping around. I was surprised how fast the band was being offered one million dollars an album. Then it got crazy. We soon had bidders from Epic and A+M offering us seven million instead. I started raising the price and before we knew it we had a ten-million-dollar deal with Elektra records. This deal was strictly for Anthrax on Elektra and I was to remain as the manager and Megaforce would no longer be the label.

As soon as the ink dried on the contract, Anthrax informed me that they were going to fire Joey. The band was at a major peak but there was also unrest within the members. It took me back to the backstage room at the Roseland just eight years prior, only this time there was a ten-million-dollar deal in the balance. Anthrax were without a singer again but this time the band had me call Joey to let him know the news which was uncomfortable for me to do. I also had to call Elektra to tell them and hope they weren't going to rip the contract up, but they supported the band's decision and the A&R man, Steve Rabowlski, really supported them and stood behind his band.

Then it was time to find a new singer. I remember in the beginning Mark Ocegueda from Death Angel and Spike Xavier from Mind Over Four were mentioned. Then there was the cattle call for lead singers at a club with an Anthrax cover band playing four songs by Anthrax over and over again while some 45 people tried out to replace Joey. Most of them were terrible and at best could maybe do vocals at an Anthrax karaoke night. It was a no brainer who everybody wanted so I made the phone call to Armored Saint vocalist John Bush. Armored Saint had been around since the early days of Thrash and John's vocals were always imitated but never equaled. I had called John once to join Metallica and he turned me down and now I was calling him to join Anthrax. I was hoping this second bolt of lightning would strike. Once he agreed to join, we knew we had found another great singer for the band. We didn't need to audition him like the rest as we knew his vocal powers and capabilities. The following year, Anthrax released *Sound of White Noise* on Elektra and the record made a big splash, just not the tidal wave Elektra was expecting. The album sold half a million copies and went Gold but Elektra had expectations the album would've sold a million copies or more.

THE BREAKUP

Marsha and I had managed Anthrax since they were little puppies all the way to the big leagues, but they never really got to experience another manager or another way of doing business. For a period of 11 years it bothered them that other bands were doing better than them. They were never sure whether it was their label or their management that hadn't made them a more popular band. However, there were many things Anthrax had to be thankful for from Crazed Management and Megaforce Records for the time we had spent together. For 11 years we performed all kinds of miracles and walked on water for Anthrax and the band always met our highest expectations ... but it was time to say goodbye to each other and part company.

Here's the scenario: After 11 years Marsha and I felt it was time to leave since our decision making was being questioned constantly. We weren't having fun anymore. This was brewing for three years. On the other hand, Anthrax had had enough of us, as well, and they truly wanted to see if there was a better world waiting for them. The only problem was I had developed a catalog that I was to get paid for if we ever parted management for perpetuity. If I quit managing the band, I would lose that. If the band fired me, I would have that. Therefore, they couldn't fire me and I couldn't quit. We both trusted our legal and accounting representatives so we asked them to arbitrate the separation agreement. We tried and succeeded in one of the fairest settlements that we both live with today. Our years as management and label for Anthrax will always be the most positive memories for Marsha and I.

THE MIND

Maria had been following the careers of vocalist-guitarist Al Jourgensen and bassist Paul Barker (of Ministry) for a while. When she introduced me to their music I was extremely impressed. Their albums *Land of Rape and Honey* and *The Mind is a Terrible Thing to Taste* were sheer genius in both production and composition. They were on Warner-Sire and had sold an excess of 100,000 units on both releases. It all happened in a true alignment of the planets type of way. Maria had suggested we sign this underground industrial band out of Ohio called Nine Inch Nails. When we went to speak to their label they weren't very interested in handing the band over but they did mention another band we would love, that being Ministry. I remember Maria talking my head up about how good Ministry was so I jumped in head-first and made the deal happen.

All everyone needed in our opinion was a good kick in the ass. Their label loved them and thought they were the greatest thing since sliced bread but there was something totally wrong with the picture. It seemed that Warner-Sire were ready to do whatever it took to break Ministry but they were scared to death of Al. They were the first to say how much they loved him but in truth they didn't have any direction as to handling the man or even carrying on a simple conversation as they were so in fear of him. When I had my early meeting with label head Seymour Stein, he told me that if I could last just six months and establish a line of communication between the label and the band he would do his best to give the forthcoming record a good shot. He asked me if I would guarantee I can last six months and I told him that would be impossible.

Next, we got on the phone with Sire's Howie Klein. The guy really knew his stuff but also needed some kind of semblance in the Ministry Camp. He also asked if Al and Paul would agree do press or radio calls to promote the new album. I wouldn't lie so I said I'd do my best at getting the guys to cooperate. Realize we still had to discuss this with the guys and from day one I realized that when you want to talk to Al you should do it eyeball to eyeball.

Meeting Al and Paul for the first time lived up to the legend. Marsha and I went to meet them at a motel lodge located near our beautiful office in Manalapan, NJ. Their room entrance was right next to a diner entrance. The door to their room was open and Paul and Al are sitting on the stoop in their underwear and boots happy to greet us. I did ask them if they were getting dressed before they visited the offices of Megaforce/CraZed Mgmnt. They obliged.

Once we got into the meeting I remember it being like a mind meld. The two of them let us know exactly where they're at. How they felt about their label, their past history, how they were basically misunderstood by most of the players in their circle. It was really serious. It was time to get an idea of what was about to come musically. Everyone in the gathering was stoked. Ministry was the only band that could really blow my mind in those days. Most of the new Metal coming out was a total rip-off from the established bands. When I needed a good dose of music it was now "Thieves" and "Stigmata" that filled the air. Even their alter ego project, The Revolting Cocks, were blowing my mind with *Beers, Steers and Queers* forever blasting in my office. CraZed Management were all in for Ministry. The first act of action was to get their production company, Hypo/Luxa, to get the rights back from their early label Wax Trax. Then it was off to meetings with everyone and anyone who had anything to do with the band at Warner and Sire.

On July 14th, 1992, *Psalm 69* was released. Ministry kept their old fans but due to the heaviness of this record it crossed over into Metal and other genres. The album had everything going for it. Every song was brilliant. Warner-Sire were overjoyed because not only did *Psalm 69* go Gold, so did Ministry's entire catalogue due to the album's success. Propelled by the first smash video for the album, "Jesus Built My Hotrod" and "New World Order," *Psalm 69* was sent soaring into Platinum sales. When it was time to tour we received an announcement to have Ministry perform at that year's second Lollapalooza music festival. The first Lollapalooza dates were a huge success in '91, featuring festival founders Jane's Addiction. The 1992 edition of the festival is what really broke it from being a one and done event. Alongside Ministry there were great acts like Red Hot Chili Peppers, Pearl Jam, Soundgarden, Ice Cube and The Jesus and Mary Chain. Ministry's appearance slot was the best in the show, next to last and just as it was starting to get dark. It was hard to convince the band to join this cavalcade of stars. Ministry liked to control the production and everything that goes on at their shows. They weren't happy to give that up to join the circus. In the end the band went down a storm every performance and their popularity grew like never before. This was a huge success for them. The next focus on the band was to break internationally, which followed from the momentum of the states. We stayed with them for about five years until we surrendered from the position while the band was touring Europe during the *Filth Pig* campaign. Al and I were working apart too much and we didn't get along well on the phone. We didn't communicate as well that way. One day things got super-heated and that was it. Much better to leave right there and not burn any bridges.

In '96 we managed Canadian Singer-Songwriter Bif Naked. We worked with Bif for five years but only had major success in Canada with two gold albums where she lived and had toured for years. At CraZed we were able to get her a recording contract at Atlantic Records but were never able to make her a household name in the USA. Unfortunately, in time we parted company but had a real hoot working with her. Bif remains a celebrity today in her Canadian homeland.

SO YOU WANT TO BE A ROCK N ROLL STAR

Just when things were mellowing out Marsha and I started getting demos from a group named DOG. The songs were eerie and emotional. There was one song in particular that blew our mind called "I Inject You." What followed was a trip to see DOG live at a club in New Jersey called The Court Tavern. We really liked them so we invited the band, a guitarist, bassist and a drum machine, to our office to discuss their future. We decided it would be best if they got a deal with a major label and were managed by CraZed.

During this time former Sire VP now Warner Reprise President Howie Klein was coming to our house in New Jersey to hang out and have some Zazula BBQ. This would be the perfect opportunity for someone to see the band live and maybe even get them signed to a record label. I remember calling the band's frontman-guitarist Michael Ferentino, at 4pm in the afternoon of that day and telling him he needed to book a show for that night. Incredibly, the band got booked for a 9pm slot at the Saint in Asbury Park. Howie had barely finished his dinner when I told him we're going to a club to see a band. It didn't take much to convince him because Howie Klein was all about the music and live shows so we got to the Saint at 8:45 that night.

Howie briefly met the band before they went on. I was very nervous but they hit it off at first meeting. The band played a 40-minute set and I was watching Klein for some sort of reaction while they played. He just sat at his table with a smile on his face. The ride home was very stressful for me. Howie asked me what were my plans and I told him I wanted to sign them to his label and have them tour, tour, tour. He said he loved them and set up a time for a meeting between me and Warner Business Affairs that very week. Howie only had one thing that made him uncomfortable: He wanted the band to lose the drum machine and get a real drummer. The band complied and brought in drummer Dave Halpern for the spot. DOG signed to Reprise and it was time to plan the album. The band also changed their name to Love in Reverse.

Howie and the band discussed producers and chose the legendary team of Russ Teitleman and Jimmy Bralower. Russ and Jeff had produced albums for Eric Clapton, George Harrison and Jeff Beck, so we knew the band was in golden hands. They were quite a power team and both had a trail of platinum albums in their wakes.

Two records came from these sessions. One was an EP, *I Was Dog*, and the second was the album *I Was*

Here. Both were released in late '95 followed by intense touring. There was no agent so the tours were basically put together by Howie Klein and I. To tell the truth we made a good team because the band were constantly on the road touring with Gravity Kills, Republica, Stabbing Westward and a full tour of the US with Ian Astbury.

Then prior to the second Reprise release, Liz Rosenberg, who at the time was Madonna's publicist, performed a miracle and got ABC's Turning Point to agree to do a special on Love in Reverse to run at 10pm on their station. You'd think this was huge. A production team followed the band all over the country. They even followed the management and band as they visited Warner and sat in on meetings and whatever to make this a killer broadcast.

The show was named "So you want to be a Rock 'n' Roll Star." It aired in front of millions of viewers in February, 1997. There was one major problem though: Love in Reverse did not take the journey to stardom. In fact, album two was treated like an albatross at the label. Only Howie Klein fought the good fight but nobody at Warner raised a hand to support the band. The TV show made the record company look like a complete failure. Instead of the show portraying a band's rise to success, it showed a band getting their hopes and dreams demolished, possibly sending them into obscurity. This turned out to be a horror story. Love in Reverse returned to their life as an indie band and we remain the dearest of friends today with Ferentino and his family.

CHAPTER 13

CRASH BANG WALLOP

1993 WAS ALL ABOUT POLYGRAM for us. We released a bunch of great non-metal records that fell on deaf ears. It seemed nothing we could do was right. We were crazy about a Funk-Metal band from Portland, Oregon, named Sweaty Nipples. We had Terry Date produce their album. He was running a hot streak at the time. Terry produced one heck of an album and we at Megaforce were stoked.

We spent a lot of money marketing the group but there were maybe three thousand sales nationwide except in one market where an amazing 10,000 were sold. That market ended up being their home state of Oregon ... go figure. It was a phenomenon and we were unable to break anywhere else with this album.

Things were not good with Polygram and we were full steam ahead at Megaforce. We were busy with Ministry, MindFunk and Anthrax on the CraZed Front.

Then, it happened.

I was committed to continue the Polygram deal for the next renewal. Marsha and I had proceeded to approve all our normal ongoing expenses. We were told all was good with our ongoing Polygram relationship and we kept spending money. At that time Megaforce was committed to spending almost four hundred thousand to our venders, promotion people, video production houses, etc. It was a heavy quarter and it was business as usual for us.

All of a sudden nobody was taking my calls at Polygram. I tried to set up a meeting and was not getting anywhere. Finally, I landed a meeting at 9:30 on a cold, dismal morning and headed from our home in Morganville, NJ to NYC, an hour away. When I got there the truth came out in the first five seconds,

"Jon, we just don't want to do this anymore."

This resounded in my head: "We just don't want to do this anymore." I was in shock. I shouldn't have been. Megaforce was not kicking ass at all and we were losing money. In fact, not only was I supposed to hear how Polygram was going to continue with us but I was supposed to pick up a check for $400,000.00 to pay my bills. The reality was brutal. Marsha and I were without funding and owed out $400,000.00. The world's heavy and brutal weight laid on me once again and I asked GOD , "Lord, what am I going to do?"

Marsha and I called every vender and told them that they would be paid in six months. We had to trim our staff and that meant letting people go. It was sad because our staff were our family. We had built all of this together and now it was ending. There was no other option. What also made me freak out a bit was my own personal bills were sky high. I spent time as a teenager homeless and on the street, built a successful business and now was losing it all in the blink of an eye. Marsha and I owned a million-dollar beach house, a 10,000 square foot office building and a nice home in NJ. All these properties carried significant costs and now every penny coming in to us was going to pay our debts and salaries instead of what we owned.

Things got so bad we were forced to sell our properties at even greater losses than we can bare to discuss and we refused to go bankrupt and instead paid every penny off. This was what followed the day Polygram said good-bye. The iceberg had hit and it was everyone for themselves. Marsha and I had the realization to sell everything and start again when I had to call my accountant about the $400,000 debt and monthly costs of my properties. That meant no office and no beach house. All I felt was total defeat. Sorrow, misery and pain consumed my mind and I was now sinking into the lowest pit of depression. Everything I worked so hard for was gone. My accountant told me to just sit back in a big chair and do not under any circumstances pick up the telephone. This was a very bad day.

Then the phone rang. Of course I didn't answer it but Marsha saw it was my father's caller ID number so she told me to take the call. She was emphatic that I get up and take the call. I wondered what it could be. I could hardly move. I was in such a terribly depressed state when I picked up the phone. An EMT was on the other line telling me my father's heart stopped beating and I better get to the Bronx immediately. I don't know how I did it but I got in the car and went flying to the Bronx to check on him. On the Raritan Bridge we got a phone call from my father's girlfriend screaming at the top of her voice range, "He's dead... he's dead." I went across four lanes of traffic to a pull off, and lost it. I was never the same from that moment on.

CARRY ON

I don't remember a lot of my life in the period that came next. I do recall that we set up shop in an 1800 square foot office space in Matawan, NJ, with a handful of staff that survived the Titanic and were here to fight another day. The records weren't selling great but by making a deal here and there we stayed alive. The only problem I had was I was so down all the time. My spark was missing. It was evident we were coasting and our greatest success came from working with Chuck Billy and Testament to release and market *Testament Live at the Fillmore* in 1995. I believe we sold around 75,000 units independently released on the Burnt Offerings label but it was quiet times other than that.

NEW HOPE PA

Marsha and I were treading water and not feeling life. We visited the charming area of Pennsylvania known as Bucks County for many years. In an attempt to find happiness, we decided to sell our home in New Jersey and move to our favorite town in Bucks County called New Hope. Marsha and I felt peace and solace there. I had money left over from the Anthrax/Elektra deal and with the sale of our NJ house we bought a huge 9,900 square foot house on 10.3 acres on one of New Hope's nicest roads. We even had an acre pond on the park-like property. This house was a great bargain. A real fixer-upper. Restoring the house to its original splendor was our goal and took my mind to a good creative place as the work started to come together. When finished it was a sight to behold, but once the work was done I started slipping again. I was having problems focusing since by this point we stopped working with both Anthrax and Ministry. Working for so many years, day in and day out, had taken its toll on me physically and mentally. I was afraid of what was to come.

TIM BURTON SAVES THE DAY

Back in October of '93, a movie came out that totally caught my attention. Tim Burton's *The Nightmare Before Christmas* had it all. The soundtrack was amazing and the characters were divine. I got lost in the movie and with every viewing I noticed something new. Something that would make me fall in love with the movie all over again. It was a great piece of art. When the first action figures came out, Marsha, who also loved the film, and I bought a set. For some reason I decided to buy every *Nightmare* toy they had in stock. We then bought a box containing 12 individual faces of Jack with each face hand molded in its own compartment. It was signed by Tim Burton and very limited. It cost us over a thousand dollars. From that point on there was a buying frenzy for everything *Nightmare*. It was crazy because I was buying 3-10 pieces of each and every item. I remember buying a lot of stuff from Japan from a company called Jun Planning. By 1995 most of my collection had grown 500% in value. My Applause Jack and Sally were worth $450.00 for the pair that originally cost $50. When it was over in and around 2005, Marsha and I catalogued over 1,000 individual pieces in our collection and we had multiples of most items.

JAMMIN

I stopped hearing voices in the middle of the night. I felt beaten and defeated. Megaforce continued with offices in the lower floor of the New Hope property. By the time we got to this status, Megaforce was more in the administration mode. We released some records but I was burnt out by then. The catalogue paid the artists and the overhead and things were okay but I was bored senseless. The best thing I did was create an arm of the company MRI to manage other labels and give them distribution under the Megaforce umbrella. This idea worked and one of our huge successes was when we took on the consulting for Sci-Fi Records who were working with the String Cheese Incident, a progressive bluegrass band from Colorado. My A&R ears perked up for the first time in years. The String Cheese Incident were ready to blow up and they did in their genre. I was thinking of the next thing to come. The whole Jam Band scene seemed to lift me out of my funk. There was a genuine musical movement going on here and I was getting into it more and more. Names like Phish, Leftover Salmon, Medeski, Martin and Wood and Moe we're getting implanted in my brain. I started going to Jam Band Festivals where I was turned onto Bela Fleck and the Flecktones, among many others. Back in New Jersey I gained an interest in a Grateful Dead sounding band called Juggling Suns. I liked the band so much I started doing shows with them as a percussionist. We made an album together for love and fun and put it on a custom label called Hydrophonic Records. The album was terribly produced and influenced by way more herbal ingestion than I care to admit. It never panned out to be anything but my relationship with the Juggling Suns was a lot of fun. It was nice being able to play the drums again and this time doing it with some stand out musicians.

Around the same time that I managed the Juggling Suns I discovered a band from up upstate New York called Ominous Seapods. We managed them and signed them to Island Records which was actually a pretty big deal. The album was great but it turned out that the Jam Band audience mainly attended concerts and tape traded with little attention spent on new releases.

So just when I started to say to myself, again, "Jon, what the hell are you doing?" BOOM! ... I thought it would never happen again but I was at the Wetlands Club in NYC and there they were. They were so great that the hairs were standing up on my arms.

THE DISCO BISCUITS

By now you readers must be thinking that "this dude lost it." "What happened to Jonny Z?" Hey, the answer is that at that time and place, *that* was where my head was at musically.

There is no real way to describe the Disco Biscuits' music. They used to joke around that they were collectively worth a million dollars' worth of college education. Their music was electronica, dance, trance, jam based, groove based, at times Zappaesque, but always genius. When we went to see the Biscuits at their first headline show after the Wetlands gig, there were five people in the audience and that included Marsha, me and my friend Steve. They played a great show in spite of the attendance. No matter how large or small their concert attendance was, each show was heavily and strategically marketed by the band. They had our total respect for their work ethic. In a short while we found ourselves managing the band and working on finding them a proper agent. They managed to stay on the road with their agent at the time but the band had all these back-end formulas that they wanted implemented when their shows were negotiated and I think they were what I called, rightfully, over demanding. They didn't mind getting paid low fees but wanted to make sure they were fairly paid if people decided to come, and they were indeed starting to come. The crowds got bigger and bigger and we all focused on breaking in the college markets. The band was then mentioned as a promising band in the Phish book and the word was getting out. The venues were getting bigger and the band sat with us to discuss their recording career. I loved the idea of a Disco Biscuit album in our catalogue so we agreed to put the record out ourselves. The guys wanted to put it out on our old Megaforce label and we did.

Their first album was self-released in 1996 by themselves and now two years later we would release their second album, *Uncivilized Area,* which was produced by Robert Hunter who at the time was producing and mixing jazz great Branford Marsalis. Rob at one time was the crazy yet amazing drummer for Raven so we had history of working together. That's right ... I was getting to work with "Wacko" once again. The second album was released in May of 1998 and the band's following was growing. Then it was time to sit down and discuss the management contract and my continuation with them.

The truth of it is, and I'm saying it here for the first time, I walked from the table. I wouldn't negotiate because I truly felt the band had learned from me and knew all my tricks. What was most certain to me was they were so super intelligent and I felt I had little to offer them and that they soon would figure out all my strategies. Also, I was getting emotionally involved and didn't want to work my heart up only for it later to be broken. I believed it was my destiny to fold early and move on. Our last involvement with the band was to help set up the first Camp Bisco festival but even that proved to us more how the band were so together and we just stepped out. To this day I believe the Disco Biscuits could emerge as one of America's greatest musical acts of all time. They just have to want it. I'm not sure but I think we parted company in 2000. On

New Year's Eve, 2018-19, The Disco Biscuits played for four nights in a row at the Fillmore in Philadelphia.

FOZZY

The last deal I did for Megaforce was to put out an album by World Champion Wrestling's Chris Jericho. The deal was made with my old friend Michael Alago who was now working for Island Records in their A&R department. It's funny, but Michael was never held in remorse by me and I genuinely adored the guy through the ages and doing business with him was always fun. So we did this Fozzy deal. I don't remember much other than this. I remember having to drive Chris to one of his matches in Trenton, N.J. from New York where Island Records had their office. For over an hour I pounded him with Lou Reed blasting from my car stereo. In an interview he did at a later date he complained about how I was such a letdown because of the music I made him listen to on that ride. I guess he wanted to listen to the old Megaforce catalog but I was feeling Lou that day!

GREAT JONES WORLD AGAIN

My good friend Robert and I started to sell off the Great Zazula toy collection in '99 and by the year 2000 moved into a retail space on Bridge Street in New Hope, PA. As mentioned earlier, Marsha and I would purchase several of each *Nightmare Before Christmas* items we found. By 1999 we figured out how to pay wholesale prices and became a full-fledged collectible store. Although it wasn't music related that's where my head was in the years from 1999 to 2004. We had loads of the rarest *Nightmare* stuff, Spawn, Living Dead Dolls, Gay Billy

Dolls—we cornered the market, Robots, Marvel and DC heroes, you name it. Only the coolest stuff graced the shelves of Great Jones World. It was a wonderful place to shop. Imagine Rock n Roll Heaven but instead of it being filled with albums it was the coolest toys and collectibles.

There was one problem. In the height of everything going well our building was sold and we were made a very handsome offer to leave. So we left and for four months ran the sale of sales. Marsha and I were tired and felt enough was enough so we officially retired and Great Jones World was no more.

CHAPTER 14

THE LAST MOSH

I N THE END OF 2000 my head was wrapped around the store Great Jones World. We took on no new clients at CraZed Management and Megaforce Records was at a point where all we did was pay royalties on the old catalogue. I had no interest in the music business. Our company MRI was successfully managing other labels and generating capital but I was totally not into it. What were we to do? My depression engulfed me and all that interested me was selling stuff. Great Jones World and the collectibles store were successful but nothing else mattered to me at that time. I worked in the store three days a week and I always enjoyed talking to my customers and selling them stuff. It was like the days I remembered and loved during Rock n Roll Heaven's heyday. It made my juices flow.

Marsha and I talked about selling Megaforce Records. What was most important to us wasn't getting the most money possible. It was most important that the company label would prevail. That it would have new energy breathed into it. We needed to sell it to someone who knew our musicians and would treat them as we did. This way, life would go on at Megaforce but now without the Z's. On July 7th, 2001, Marsha and I sold Megaforce, stepping away but allowing the name and catalogue to live on, to our loyal employee Missi Collazo who was running the affairs of the company at that time. Marsha and I made this decision and never looked back.

In the years that followed Marsha and I worked at the store in New Hope which lasted until January of 2004. My mind wasn't all that good after '04 and I pretty much treaded water for a period of 8 years and enjoyed our Bucks Country life during that time.

SANDY RELIEF BENEFIT

On May 11th, 2013, Marsha and I felt like stepping up to do something to help raise money for the victims of Hurricane Sandy. We missed our roots and wanted to do something in the old neighborhood for a while and kept on hearing that the money raised for The Sandy victims was taking its sweet time reaching the people, so we figured we can turn the money over to the people in less than a week if we raised it. We teamed up with a local 501c3 organization and got the ball rolling.

We were able to get a venue for the show in Freehold, NJ, and it was lineup time next.

Right away I called my oldest friends to see if they were free for May 11th. Anvil- Free. Raven- Free. Who next? I asked Metal Joe from the Old Bridge Militia Foundation who he would like us to bring to the lineup and he said to us, The Rods. The OBMF is an organization put together by Rock'n Ray Dill and Metal Joe Chimienti to help kids with scholarships who would not be able to get music lessons or buy instruments. The Foundation was happy to come support the benefit show. The Old Bridge Metal Militia officially became the Old Bridge Metal Foundation at the show that night .

I called Carl Canedy and told him about the cause and invited the Rods if they were available and they were. Next up was a miracle. We asked TT Quick to close the show and they too were open that night. WOW! What a lineup. Raven, Anvil, The Rods and TT Quick. Everyone once again doubted me and told me 2000 people are not coming to see that bill alone. Meanwhile seats sold daily. I don't remember where it came from but I ended up on the phone with JJ French discussing the fact that if we wanted Twisted Sister on the bill, Dee goes on at 10:00. All other details were worked out and Twisted Sister were now headlining the show as special guests.

In the end we sold a lot of tickets and we gave 100% of the money to the Sandy Victims, as promised, within days of the show. One of the most fulfilling feelings was being able to help these people especially since so many had supported us in the clubs in the early days. I want to thank Under My Skin, The Old Bridge Militia Foundation and a special thanks to John D and John Albino for making this show a huge success. This was a great pleasure for Marsha and I.

Later that year I made a stab at re-entering the music business with my lifelong friends Maria Ferrero and Chuck Billy. We formed a company named Breaking Bands which handled the business affairs of Exodus, Shattered Sun and Soilwork during its short life. I just didn't have my old drive anymore and Marsha's health became an issue so we opted out of the business. Before my final retirement I worked with England's Venom Inc. and was able to get them both recording and publishing deals. They also did a great run of shows during this time period throughout the world. Not bad for agreeing to give some old Legends some advice.

We knew the time would come and in June of 2018 I asked the boys if they'd mind me permanently retiring. It was enough. I proved to myself that I still had the sparkle, but at 66 years of age it was officially over. This time there would be no turning back.

Today we live in Florida and my phone still rings consistently with people asking me the answers to those unanswerable questions. I love to help but even I plan to cut that down and just focus on living out the rest of our days the best we can.

Remember...

"NOTHING TO IT BUT TO DO IT"

I'm sure our paths will cross at some great Metal show somewhere, look for us in the crowd.

On January 23rd, 2019 Marsha and I were honored with a Lifetime Achievement Award and Induction into The Hall of Heavy Metal History.

FINAL TAKE

Those who Rocked who were left out unintentionally:

Icon - they were a great band from Arizona. Ed Trunk signed them to Megaforce/Avalanche. On Aug 24, 1989 they released Right Between the Eyes. We felt we had a substantial radio friendly record with Icon and tried to compete with the big powers at radio. We were crushed and would only attempt harder and heavier Metal in the future for the Mega-Roster

Skatenigs - put out Stupid *People Shouldn't Breed* on Megaforce. These guys were great live. I spent some crazy times with them in Austin and their album was Produced by Al Jourgensen. I thought the band was ahead of its time.

Tad - Thomas Doyle and company were probably the sweetest and funniest musicians we ever dealt with. We simply loved just hanging with Tad. They were a Seattle Sub-Pop band that we got signed to East West/ Elektra and they released one great album, *Infrared Riding Hood,* in 1995. Under our management they toured the US and Europe with Soundgarden at the peak of Soundgarden's career. Tad Doyle and Co. still thrive in Seattle to this day

Hotel Hunger - Nobody would listen to this band at radio so we leaked it as a demo that was mis-shipped from a very famous band. I'd like to think it had Keith Richards written on it. I may be all wrong. The tape with the name came in a Walkman Cassette player queued to the song. Crazy, right? The band were amazing and from Denmark. Atlantic Records thought I had gone insane. The band sounded like a pop band. I always thought U2 meets Simple Minds. Atlantic wanted METAL. Even I don't remember what prompted me other than I loved the band and my office was crazy about them.

Prophet - They released Cycle of the Moon in the later part of the Mega-Atlantic era. Once again we tried to get some hi-quality Rock on the airwaves and miserably failed. Prophet was a band with a Super-Star New Jersey lineup of musicians and their album was produced by Spencer Proffer of Quiet Riot.

Milc - Milc were one of the most interesting bands that we dealt with. They were brought to us in 1989 by managing assistant Jim Lewi through Alex Perialas who thought this band was the cat's meow. We had a demo produced by Robert Hunter and guest producer Branford Marsalis for one song and excitedly brought their music to Atlantic. Unfortunately, Atlantic was pressing me for *Metal* and had no interest in the band. Now please understand that when Phish played N.Y. they opened for Milc and vice versa in Vermont. I later laughed when Dave Mathews Band broke. We had that sound maybe first with Milc. When Atlantic turned them down we went to every A+R person under the sun to come see the band but they all passed. What a crying shame. After an awful lot of work and effort there was much frustration and disappointment on both sides and like the red sea we parted,

Fear Nuttin Band - I saw this band at a National Battle of the Bands where they finished in second place. We recorded an album together with producer Terry Date but again we were too ahead of our times. Hailing from Springfield, Massachusetts, they still perform to this day and released *Yardcore* in 2008.

The Vincent Black Shadow - were a great band from Vancouver, Canada. We handled their affairs in the United States. The band released the album *Fears in The Water* under our watch in 2008. One of the great Kirkham brothers, who co-founded this group, Chris, performs as Nim Vind today.

Shattered Sun - Shattered Sun are from Corpus Christi, Texas who were discovered by Maria Ferrero and was managed by Breaking Bands. They released their album *Hope Within Hatred* under our guidance. Chuck Billy still manages the band today.

Soilwork - Soilwork were also managed by Breaking Bands. They released three albums under our watch. Bjorn Strid and I have become dear friends in the present days.

Venom Inc. - The Venom love story has gone on for over 35 years. Mantas and Bray stayed in touch but it wasn't until Tony "Demolition Man" Dolan got a hold of me that things started cooking again. After their success at Europe's Keep It True Festival word got back to me that the magic was more than back in the Venom Camp. I contacted Dolan and Mantas to see what's up and 3 months later they were in the studio recording an album for Nuclear Blast. The band toured the planet twice under my watch with little time off. It was starting to feel good but when I found out that Marsha's health wasn't all that good and felt at the same time that I was starting to get too stressed out I kindly asked the boys if I could take a permanent hiatus in May of 2018. The band went straight away to a string of US shows and some special dates with Glenn Danzig right after our departure.

The Absence - I love this band. Their drummer is Jeramie Kling in Venom Inc. They released, *A Gift for the Obsessed*, in 2018 and it's a killer album. If you want a Metal album that's in your face with killer musicianship this is it.

Wizards of Winter - I managed this Holiday Production for 2 years. It is hoped that in the two years they learned from me and were able to use this knowledge in dealing with their future endeavors. We parted company in 2016 and the band has had continued success with 2019 being their best season yet. I'm very fond of Scott and Sharon (the band leaders) to this day.

John's Crossing/Insite Music - This is a strange one to explain but the story has merit. John Albino and I have known each other over 20 years. He and I chose different paths in life but just prior to May11, 2015 I contacted John to help me produce the Benefit for the victims of Super Storm Sandy. He complied and as you know the show was a huge success. Albino and I spent much time on the phone discussing the show and whenever we could get a chance we would discuss religion. John and I spent much time discussing Jesus. John at that time was very involved in his church and would on occasion run worship on Sundays for part of the service. In fact, it was at a Sunday picnic for the church where I first heard his music live. After that we discussed making an album of music dedicated to the Lord. The album, *John's Crossing* was released in October of 2017. I stayed in New Jersey for most of the albums recording. It was released on Insite Records, its own label, whose mission was to spread the word and give testimony. The experience was extremely spiritual and one that is close in my heart to this day. At the moment Insite Records is based in Matawan NJ and John's Crossing are in the studio recording album two.

Blessed Death - Before I close I have to make special mention of a record deal that was between Tungsten Records and Megaforce. Tungsten was owned by the famed Ray Dill and Joe Chimiente from the Old Bridge Militia and it was these folk who brought us the band Blessed Death . Now I don't quite remember any crazy stories about this signing but I can tell you that the band was really Heavy and it would be great to see them at a Reunion show back in NJ

And just to go on record there was an **Eric Steele** album and we released the first two **Gravedigger** albums here in the states .

And yes there was one more band worth mentioning. They were **Goud's Thumb** a band we signed from Portland Maine.

If we missed anyone else I'm truly sorry.

EPILOGUE

I'VE CHOSEN TO PEN THIS epilogue to Jon's memoir for many reasons, but mostly because: *Many,* may think, boy, did he get lucky, or maybe he was nuts, and the answer is *yes*, he was both. Lucky, because he could believe so strongly that anything is possible, and nuts, because in every brilliant man there is a bit of crazy. That is what propels them to reach out and go for the stars.

Many of the stories here may sound far-fetched but I assure you they're all real. He, along with a cast of characters, gave up days and nights or added weeks-worth of hours in order to make the impossible possible. I could have never dreamt this journey would be my life but it was and it is and I'm forever grateful to have it.

—Marsha Zazula

MEGAFORCE AND ZAZULA DISCOGRAPHY

1983

Venom- Die Hard/Acid Queen
Metallica- Kill 'Em All (July 25th)
Manowar- Into Glory Ride (July 1st)
Raven- All For One (August 25th)
Mercyful Fate- Black Masses/Black Funeral
Mercyful Fate- Melissa
Metallica- Whiplash
Anthrax- Soldiers Of Metal

1984

Metallica- Jump In The Fire
Anthrax- Fistful Of Metal (February 2nd)
Exciter- Violence And Force (February 27th)
TT Quick- TT Quick (April 24th)
Born To Metalize- Compilation (May 1st)
Eric Steel- Eric Steel (May 10th)
Metallica- Ride the Lightning (July 27th)
Gravedigger- Heavy Metal Breakdown (October 20th)

Raven- Live At The Inferno (November 1st)
Blue Cheer- The Beast Is Back

1985

Anthrax- Armed And Dangerous (February 15th)
From The Megavault- Compilation (April 1st)
Blessed Death- Kill Or Be Killed (April 1st)
Gravedigger- Witch Hunter (May 10th)
S.O.D- Speak English Or Die (August 30th)
Lone Rager- Metal Rap (August 5th)
Overkill- Feel The Fire (October 15th)
Anthrax- Spreading The Disease (October 30th)

1986

TT Quick- Metal Of Honor (February 14th)

1987

Overkill- Taking Over (February 23rd)
Anthrax- Among The Living (March 22nd)
Testament- The Legacy (April 21st)
Ace Frehley- Frehley's Comet (April 27th)
Power Chords Vol.1- Compilation (August 10th)
M.O.D- U.S.A For M.O.D (September 24th)
Anthrax- I'm The Man E.P
Overkill- Fuck You E.P (November 13th)
Testament- Live at Eindhoven

1988

Prophet- Cycle Of The Moon (January 1st)
Frehley's Comet- +1 (February 2nd)
King's X- Out Of The Silent Planet (March 28th)
Frehley's Comet- Second Sighting (May 24th)
Testament- The New Order (May 5th)

Overkill- Under The Influence (July 5th)
M.O.D- Surfin' M.O.D (July 25th)
John Bayless- Greetings From John Bayless (September 10th)
Anthrax- State Of Euphoria (September 19th)

1989

M.O.D- Gross Misconduct (February 10th)
Hotel Hunger- This Is Where The Fun Starts (May 8th)
Trust- Live Paris By Night (May 22nd)
King's X- Gretchen Goes To Nebraska (June 27th)
Testament- Practice What You Preach (August 4th)
Icon- Right Between The Eyes (August 28th)
Anthrax- Penikufesin
Ace Frehley- Trouble Walkin' (October 13th)
Overkill- The Years Of Decay (October 17th)

1990

Vio-lence- Oppressing The Masses (July 30th)
Anthrax- Persistence Of Time (August 21st)
Testament- Souls Of Black (October 9th)
King's X- Faith Hope Love (October 23rd)

1991

Overkill- Horrorscope (September 3rd)
Vio-lence- Torture Tactics
Deeper into the Vault
Anthrax- Attack of The Killer B's
Mindfunk- Mindfunk (March 12th)

1992

Skatenigs- Stupid People Shouldn't Breed
SOD: Stormtrooper Of Death- Live At Budokan

Skatenigs- Loudspeaker

1993

Nudeswirl- Nudeswirl
Tribe After Tribe- Love Under Will
Sweaty Nipples- Sweaty Nipples
Warren Haynes- Tales of Ordinary Madness
Mindfunk- Dropped

1997

Juggling Suns- Living On The Edge of Change

1998

The Ominous Seapods- Matinee Idols: Late Show
Disco Biscuits- Uncivilized Area (May 19th)

2000

Fozzy- Fozzy (October 24th)

2001

Disco Biscuits- They Missed The Perfume (April 3rd)

2015

Wizards of Winter- Magic of Winter (November)

2017

John's Crossing- Self Titled (October)

ACKNOWLEDGMENTS

Mega-thanks to those whose hands touched the making of the dream

God, Marsha Zazula, Danielle Zazula, Rikki Zazula Blaire Brewer, Evan Zazula, Robert Zazula, Richard Lin, Maria Ferrero, Brian "Buy or Die" Nyers, Anthony and Gabrielle Incigeri, Ray Dill, Metal Joe Chimiente, Bulldozer Bob, Bobby Oujo, Gregory Moench, The Old Bridge Militia, Nat and Hedy Tehrani, William Rutenberg, William Leibowitz, Chuck Billy, Ed Trunk, Gary Waldman, Mary Lyne, Missi Callazo, Michael Buchman, Jessica Harley, Art Ring, Phil Hardy, John Warden, Bill, "Ostrogoth" Ketch, Mike Mazer, Victoria Minervini, Murray Richman, Eileen Genna, Nancy Niles, Michelle Fuehrer, Deidra Locassio, Alicia De Senna, Jim Lewi, Lisa Wisenewski, Greg Caputo, Chris Rake, Maria Vesce, Harold and Shari Risch, Jeff Rowland, John Jackson, Chris Blackwell, Doug Morris, David Glew, Phil Cooper, Debbie from Island UK, Janet Kleinbaum, Bill Berger, Rick Bleiweicz, Kevin Lyman, Jason Flom, Larry Yasgar, Bill Elson, John Dittmar, Alex Perialas, John Perialas, Carl Canedy, Mel Lewinter, Holly Ferguson, Mary Hooten, Jan and Jane from Fair Warning, Paul Curcio, Mike Faley, Eddie Kramer, Terry Date, Mark Dodson, Chris Bubacz, Cees Wessel, Michael Toorock, Michael Mitnick, Judy Bray, Tom Kolinchak, Nick Gordon, Michael Wagener, Robert Hunter, Tim Borror, Mike van Risjwijk and Aardshok Magazine ,Metal Hammer Magazine, Kerrang Magazine, Metal Forces Magazine, Burn Magazine, All the other metal mags and fanzines ,Geoff Gordon, Brian Dillworth, Dan Rozenblum, Jim Kozlowski, Janine Small, Jane Gehraty, Frank Barcelona, Ed Micone, Phil Ernst, Marsha Vlasic, George and Mike Parente, Richard Saunders, Fat Harry, Marc Reiter, Mike Alago, Juergen Wiggenhaus, Steve Rabowski, Howie Klein, Seymour Stein, Tunc Erim, Ahmet Ertegun, Michael Mitnick, Judy Bray, Rick Krim, Ralph Simon, Keith Wood, Dave Wood, Martin Hooker, Steve Mason, Bob Chippiardi, Walter O'Brien, Kevin Hodapp, Gene Ambo, Mark Weiss, Frank White, Fritch Clark, Ron Akiyama, Uwe Buffo Schnaddelbach, George Chin, Matthias Prill, Tracey Rayfield, Tiffany Billy, Rick Downey, George Geranius, Rod Smallwood, Andy Taylor, Alex Kochen, Barry Drinkwater, Keith Drinkwater, Steve Miles, Ron Boutwell, Far Sakota, David, Tan, Ko Sakai, Jaap Wanamaker, Yorck Eisel, Dean Halterman, Munsey Ricci, Bill Graham, Jim Cardillo, KJ Doughton, Ron Quintana, Xavier Russel, Malcome Dome, Monte Conner, Howard Johnson, Geoff Barton, Bernard Doe, Bob Muldowney, Lonn Friend, Bernie Borvoisin, Nono Krief, Christian Lamet, Brian Lew, Bob Nalbandian, Brie Gentry and Annette Lopez-Lamott.

Harold Claros-Maldonado would like to thank: Mom, my Claros/Maldonado family in the USA and Bolivia, MetallicA, Lopes/Nguyen Family, Ayush Rohatgi, Brian Baynes, Michael Feldmann, Marcus Preston, my friends worldwide and all the current (good) independent labels, record stores, musicians, artist, photographers and fans keeping this *current* punk, hardcore and metal scene alive, healthy and thriving-

FOREVER STRONGER THAN ALL

A WORD FROM HAROLD

Music was always an integral part of my upbringing. My parents, Bolivian immigrants, would play Bolivian folk music, Luis Miguel, D.L.G or my mother's favorite, Marc Anthony. I learned from an early age that music had a power over me unlike anything else did. It wasn't until I was 10 when I saw Wayne's World that I discovered Heavy Metal and by middle school I was already listening to Metallica, Anthrax, Megadeth and Slayer. I had become an *outcast*.

Throughout my early musical research, I would come across the label *Megaforce Records* on many of the records I would pick up or in band's linear notes thanking *Jon and Marsha Z*. I knew that these two people were in charge of spearheading this thrash movement but knew very little about them. As the years passed my admiration and loyalty to the *Megaforce Records* catalog grew exponentially, with my interest expanding to S.O.D, Vio-lence and Testament. I would wear a *Ride the Lightning* t-shirt in high school while drawing the album cover for *Spreading the Disease* in my sketchbook disappearing from the world. That shirt was almost like a body armor for me, attracting only the few other freaks and geeks that attended my high school. As teenagers we would drink and worship this music playing loudly through our speakers, having "teenage intellectual" conversations and debates such as, *which band is more true to hardcore? S.O.D or M.O.D? or Cliff Burton vs. Frank Bello?*

When I flew to Orlando to meet Jon and Marsha we clicked instantly. Jon and I found ourselves over-talking each other which is quite a feat to do. It's something I quickly learned that happens when you have two chatterboxes in Jon and myself. As Jon spoke, Marsha was the wise Yoda like figure who spoke seldom but always with a weight of seriousness behind it. A calm, collected and warm person who spoke to me like I was already family. I noticed right there and then the magic that is the Zazula's. Jon would talk you to the cosmos while Marsha would safely land you on the moon. It's a great partnership and one that's worked out for more than 30 years effectively.

It was Jon and Marsha that believed in the young bands they signed and worked with. The ones who put their own money, timeless hours and worked it into existence. That's how they operate, its symmetry, equal on both ends. Through this partnership they've had they've helped to shape and direct Heavy Metal into what it is today. Their music is *still* relevant and important. It's not something of the past that has no place in today's scene, the current scene is derivative of these *Megaforce Records* releases!

Just last month I went to see a local Richmond d-beat band Nosebleed at a basement show. While their guitarist was tuning his guitar he went into the S.O.D., *March of The S.O.D.,* riff. It sounded crispy and crunchy like it had been written today. Then yesterday at Richmond's hardcore festival United Blood local thrashers Enforced covered Vio-lence, *Liquid Courage.* The entire club erupted as fist were being smashed into faces violently. To think that 30 years later musicians of today would cover these songs would probably be unimaginable. That's what good music does though, its timeless while being relevant to the current scene.

Jon and Marsha had the *foresight* others didn't. They had the courage and drive to invest in these young bands, their albums, schedule tours and produce quality merchandise. It's the classic American dream of starting a family business with your spouse and making an empire out of those humble beginnings. Together Jon and Marsha built a fucking dynasty out of that symmetry they share and I'm thankful like many other fans for it!

—Harold Claros-Maldonado. April 7th, 2019

Printed in the USA
CPSIA information can be obtained
at www.ICGtesting.com
LVHW080807090124
768424LV00012B/1049